Explaining
The Second
Coming

J. David Pawson, M.A., B.Sc.

Sovereign World

Scripture quotations are taken from
The Holy Bible, New International Version.
© Copyright 1973, 1978, 1984 International Bible Society.
Published by Hodder & Stoughton.

ISBN: 1 85240 118 4

SOVEREIGN WORLD LIMITED
P.O. Box 777, Tonbridge, Kent TN11 9XT, England.

Contents

A Word of Introduction

Our attitude to the future is ambiguous, a mixture of fear and fascination. We want to know what is going to happen to us and the rest of the human race – and we don't want to know! Were it possible, which one of us would wish to learn the date of our death or the end of the world?

We are the first generation to live with the possibility that these two dates might coincide. In one survey half the teenagers believed their death and the death of our planet would be simultaneous. Whether through nuclear holocaust (a diminishing fear) or environmental pollution (a growing fear), the days of life on earth seem to be numbered.

Again, our reaction is inconsistent, even contradictory. On the one hand, many try to forget the future and squeeze as much purpose and pleasure out of the present as possible. *'Let us eat and drink, for tomorrow we die'* (this is actually in the Bible! Isaiah 22:13, quoted in 1 Corinthians 15:32). 'Existentialism' is the name for this philosophy of life and it is widespread.

On the other hand, there is more interest in the future and efforts to change it than ever before, an enthusiasm that hovers on the border of panic. Attitudes cover a wide spectrum from elated optimism to depressed pessimism, sometimes swinging wildly from one extreme to the other, from faith to fatalism.

Broadly speaking, there are three ways in which we can pierce the veil that hides the future from us.

First, the *superstitious* method. Divination is an ancient practice, but still very much alive. Clairvoyants and mediums, crystal balls and ouija boards, tarot cards and tea-leaves – there are many forms. Six out of ten men and seven out of ten women read their horoscopes every day; no popular newspaper or magazine would dare to neglect the stars.

Yet it has been estimated that none of these channels has ever been more than 5% accurate, which means that they are at least 95% mistaken. Only those willing or wanting to be deceived forget the errors and focus on the few fulfilments.

Second, the *scientific* method. Deduction from observation is the basic tool of modern science. To calculate present trends and project them is the concern of 'futurology', as the technique is now named. Professorial chairs in the subject are being established in universities, particularly those majoring in technology. Industrial, commercial and political spheres have their 'think-tanks'. More than one computer programme has calculated the likely date of the end of the world as 2040 (by taking into account population growth, food and energy resources, environmental decay, etc.).

Average accuracy of published results has so far been around 25% or, to put it negatively, up to 75% wrong. The short-term forecasts, as one would expect, are much more reliable than the long-term ones.

Third, the *scriptural* method. Declaration about future events is a major feature of the Bible. It claims to contain the words of God (*'Thus says the Lord'* occurs 3808 times!), the only person who is in a position to *'make known the end from the beginning, from ancient times, what is still to come'* (Isaiah 46:10). Over a quarter of all the verses in the Bible contain a prediction about the future. Altogether 737 separate forecasts are made, from some only mentioned once to others hundreds of times.

Of these, 594 (over 80%) have already come true. Since those that have not are all concerned with the end of the world, which obviously has not happened yet, the Bible has actually achieved 100% accuracy. All that could have taken place already has done so, which should be ample grounds for confidence that the rest will also be fulfilled. (These statistics, with a detailed analysis of every prediction, may be found in the 'Encyclopedia of Biblical Prophecy' by J. Barton Payne, Hodder and Stoughton, 1973.)

How astonishing then that people would rather consult satanic rigmarole or human reason than divine revelation. Part of the blame must lie at the door of the Church, which has neither been clear nor confident enough in sharing her knowledge, the result of allowing scientific scepticism about the supernatural to undermine the authority of scripture.

The Bible reveals its secrets to those who read it with reverence and obedience, in a humble and teachable spirit. It yields more to simple intelligence than sophisticated intellectualism. It is written for ordinary people in ordinary language (New Testament Greek is taken from the streets, not the classics). It is meant to be taken at face value and taken seriously. When it is, a clear picture of the future emerges.

Many things are predicted – personal and political, social and environmental, moral and meteorological. But one event stands out above them all: the return to this world of a person who lived here two thousand years ago, a carpenter from the village of Nazareth. Were he simply a human being, this would seem unbelievable. If he was what he claimed to be, divine as well as human, the one and only God-man, his return becomes credible and congruous. Rejected by an unbelieving world, it is only right that he should be publicly vindicated.

This event is more frequently predicted than any other and dominates the biblical preview. The question: 'What is the world coming to?' is changed into: 'Who is the world coming to?' or, better still: 'Who is coming to the world?'

History will be brought to a conclusion. And by a human being. Not by pressing the button of a nuclear attack on earth but by breaking the seals of a scroll in heaven on which is already written the countdown of world events (Revelation 5:1, 6:1). At the climax of the crisis, Jesus himself will reappear on the world stage to take personal control of the grand finale.

Such is the heart of the Christian hope for the future. Jesus is the only hope, the only person with sufficient ability and authority, character and compassion, to right the wrongs of this sick, sad and sinful world. On his first visit to our planet he demonstrated that he *could* do it; on his second he has promised that he *will* do it.

In theory, the Church of Jesus Christ gives his return a central place. The most regularly repeated creeds, the Apostles' and the Nicene, include it as a fundamental part of the faith. Bread and wine are regularly taken as a reminder of his former presence and current absence *'until he comes'* (1 Corinthians 11:26). The liturgical calendar includes Advent in December, the first part of which anticipates his return.

In practice, however, neglect of this vital truth is spreading. Even during Advent, any thought about his second coming is quickly forgotten in the celebration of his first, in the festivities of Christmas. Some have become so confused or impatient with the doctrinal differences over it that they have taken refuge in agnosticism on the subject. More have conformed to the world's obsession with the present by concentrating on the application of Christian insights and efforts to the personal and political needs of the day.

Now abideth faith, hope and love; but the weakest of these is hope!

That is a tragedy in a world of widespread depression and despair. The Bible describes unbelievers as *'without hope and without God in the world'* (Ephesians 2:12). In such darkness, Christians should be shining beacons of hope. After all, they are the only ones who know how it will all end. They know that it will all end well, that good will triumph over evil, that their Lord will defeat the devil, that the Kingdom of God will come on earth as it is in heaven.

This hope is *'an anchor for the soul, firm and secure'* (Hebrews 6:19). The raging storm of world events will get worse rather than better, until every part of the globe is affected. May the reading of this little book help you to get your anchor down now!

1

Making Sense Of
His Return

With over three hundred references to the second coming in the
New Testament, the problem is almost too much material rather
than too little. Fitting it all together feels like assembling a jigsaw
puzzle with interchangeable pieces.

Perhaps this explains why there are such differences of
understanding, even among Christians with implicit confidence in
scripture. They all agree on the central fact of his coming, but
disagree strongly about what precedes and what follows that event.

Rather than add yet another chart or time schedule to the many
already published, this study will take a topical approach. The
data will be collected under five basic questions:

Who – will he come as the pre-existent Son of God or the
incarnate Son of Man?

Where – will he come to the whole world at once or just to
one place in it?

How – will the second coming be like the first or totally
different?

When – will he come soon and suddenly or only after clear
signals?

Why – what can he only achieve by coming back here, and
how long will it take?

Some of the answers may come as a surprise, even a shock, to
those who have only been exposed to one school of thought or

have already got fixed ideas on the subject. Readers coming with an open mind and an open Bible will get the most benefit.

Who?

Who has not continued gazing into the distance long after a train or plane has taken a loved one out of sight, especially if that is expected to be a final parting? Is it a reluctance to acknowledge the departure, an attempt to postpone the pain? We are not so likely to do it if we are sure we shall see that person again, that they will return from their journey.

This is exactly what happened to the men of Galilee when Jesus went up into the clouds, less than two months after he came back to them from the dead. Long after he disappeared, they were still staring at the point of their final glimpse. It took two angels to reassure them and bring their attention down to earth again.

They assured the disciples that he *would* return, implying that they would not see him again until then. What interests us is the phrase they used: '**This same Jesus** ...*will come back*' (Acts 1:11).

Two things are worth noting. First they used his human name, not any of his divine titles. Second, they emphasised that he will not have changed in the meantime.

One of our common fears is that during a long separation persons may change so much that a former relationship cannot be resumed. Disciples of Jesus need not worry. They may change, indeed should change for the better, but he neither will nor needs to. He is '*the same yesterday and today and for ever*' (Hebrews 13:8).

It cannot be too strongly emphasised that the divine Christ and the human Jesus are one and the same person. Both conscious attempts and unconscious impressions have driven a wedge between them. Even in Christian circles it has been assumed that the Son of God was only made flesh, 'incarnated', for thirty-three years and has now 'gone back' to his former state.

The truth is that he became human and keeps his resurrected body for the rest of eternity. He has retained his humanity. He is the only mediator between God and man precisely because he is still '*the man*' (1 Timothy 2:5). That is why he is the perfect high priest, who can both sympathise with us and represent us before God (Hebrews 4:15). Incredibly, a perfect human being is now in control of the universe (Matthew 28:18)!

We must not forget that this person, who has 'ascended' to the highest heaven is the same one who 'descended' to lowest earth (Ephesians 4:9-10). The place of his baptism is, in fact, the lowest point on the earth's surface!

The exalted was first humbled – as a baby in Bethlehem, a boy in Nazareth. He was a wood-worker for eighteen years, then a wonder-worker for three (the same proportion of six to one as his heavenly father; Genesis 1). The latter period made him famous among his people, the focus of attention for friends and enemies alike. His ignominious death at an early age was terribly public.

All this meant that he was widely known and well-known. Of course, there were varying degrees of intimacy, different circles of acquaintance. Thousands listened to him; seventy were commissioned to spread his mission; twelve were chosen to follow him; three shared unique experiences with him (Peter, James and John at the transfiguration for example); one was closer than any other (John, the 'beloved', into whose care Jesus entrusted his bereaved mother).

This human knowledge of the human Jesus is enshrined in the four Gospels. From these emerges a clear portrait of a unique personality, loved by sinners, hated by hypocrites, adored by the poor and feared by the powerful. His eyes could fill with tears of compassion for the oppressed and blaze with anger against the oppressor. His hands could lift the fallen and whip the greedy. His tongue could be softer and sharper than any other.

It is this Jesus who will return to the planet earth one day. He will not have changed. He will be no less human than he was when walking the dusty roads, reclining at meal tables, sleeping in a boat, riding a donkey or washing feet.

However, it must be pointed out that there had already been one major change in his humanity even before he left the earth. God gave him a new body when he raised him out of the tomb (for fuller details, see my "Explaining the Resurrection" in this series).

This 'glorious body' (Philippians 3:21) has the same appearance, even to the disfigurements of the crucifixion with scars on the head, back, side, hands and feet. But it was no longer subject to the 'natural' processes of aging, decay and death. When he returns it will be no older, still in its prime, still thirty-three – except that his hair will be snow-white (Revelation 1:14; a symbol of his sharing the nature of his Father, the 'Ancient of Days'; Daniel 7:13).

This transformation of his body did not make Jesus less human but more human, which is what God had intended all human beings to be and, by his grace what many will be. In this Jesus is our 'pioneer' (Hebrews 2:10), blazing a trail for us to follow. But he will not leave us to find our own way; he will come back and take us to be with him, for he himself is *'the way'* (John 14:3-6).

Then we too will have 'glorious bodies' just like his. But we will be the same persons we have always been (which is why Christians speak about 'resurrection' rather than 'reincarnation'; popular usage of the latter implies a change of identity).

We need to remember that Jesus was not always a human being. Indeed, he was not always 'Jesus'; that was a name he acquired when he was incarnate, embodied, and when he became human (Matthew 1:21). Unlike us he existed before he was conceived, and was the only person who ever chose to be born. He was the eternal Son of God, the Lord of glory, the Word. He was the divine being before he was a human being.

It is therefore very significant that the angels used his human name when promising his return to planet earth. It is the *'Son of man'* who will appear in the clouds (Daniel 7:13; Mark 14:62). It is the embodied Jesus who will return to planet earth, not some intangible apparition of the son of God (Daniel 3:25).

Some, finding such a 'bodily' return difficult to accept, have 'spiritualised' his coming, identifying it with the 'coming' of his Spirit to the church at Pentecost or his 'coming' to each individual believer at conversion. But neither of these interpretations does justice to the promise that *'this **same** Jesus will come back'*.

The Jesus who invited the disciples to touch him, who ate fish in their presence, who walked to Emmaus and broke bread, who told Thomas to examine his wounds, who cooked breakfast on the shores of Galilee – it is this Jesus who will return one day.

But we must face one implication of believing this: an embodied Jesus can only be in one place on earth at once. Even with his glorious resurrection body he could only be in Emmaus or Jerusalem or Galilee. He never appeared in two places at the same time.

Therefore, when he returns to this earth, he can only come to one geographical location. Where will that be?

Where?

If the return of Jesus is 'physical', it must also be local. His Spirit can be everywhere, but his body must be somewhere. Before he ascended, Jesus could not be in two places at once.

That is why he told the disciples it was for their good that he was leaving them and sending another 'stand-by' to take his place (John 16:7). He had promised to be with them always, even to the end of the age (Matthew 28:20); yet they would be *scattered* to the ends of the earth (Acts 1:8). The only way he could do this was to remove his body and replace his physical presence with his ever-present and omnipresent Spirit, unlimited by time or space.

This situation will not be reversed when he returns. Believers will not lose his Spirit but will enjoy his physical presence as well. They will be doubly blessed!

However, since his body, like ours, must always be at one point on the surface of the earth, his return means that his disciples will have to be *gathered* together from every part of the globe. Only thus could they experience his bodily presence. This is precisely what the New Testament promises will happen.

So where will he appear? Where will his people gather to welcome him?

Cities compete to host such prestigious events as the Olympic games. Which of them will have the honour of greeting the King of kings? Will it be one of the political capitals – Washington, Beijing, Brussels or Delhi? Will it be one of the financial centres – New York, Tokyo, London or Hong Kong? Will it be one with ecclesiastical fame – Rome, Geneva or Canterbury?

13

It will be none of these. They may be important to men but are not significant for God. He chose for his capital a most unlikely city, hidden in the hills, away from roads and rivers, an obscure mountain refuge that would be unknown had not God chosen to attach his name to it. Even today the nations of the world will not recognise it, by refusing to open embassies there. It has known more conflict and tragedy than any other and may yet prove the spark to ignite a conflagration throughout the Middle East.

The most important happenings in human history took place there; they divided time into two parts – B.C. and A.D. It was there that the only Son of God was unjustly executed for crimes he had never committed, actually bearing the sins of the whole world. It was there that he defeated the last enemy, death, becoming the first person to have an immortal body.

It is from this city that he departed to return to his home in heaven and it is to this city that he will return from heaven. He called it *'the city of the Great King'* (Matthew 5:35). It is the city he wept over, telling its citizens they would not see him again until they said *'Blessed is he who comes in the name of the Lord'* (Matthew 23:37-39, quoting one of the 'Hallel' psalms sung by Jerusalem pilgrims to welcome their 'Messiah').

The history of this city is by no means over. Future events are unveiled in the book of Revelation, where it is described as *'the great city'* (11:8) and *'the city he loves'* (20:9). It is to this city that the nations will one day turn for the arbitration of international disputes, enabling multilateral disarmament (Isaiah 2:1-4); Micah 4:1-5). For this is Jerusalem, or 'Zion', where the Lord will reign.

The city is strategically placed for an international function. It is quite literally at the very centre of the world's land mass and at the meeting-point of three continents – Europe, Africa and Asia. It would seem an ideal rendezvous for the gathering of Jesus' followers.

But how many will there be, bearing in mind that the crowd will include Christians who have already died and are then raised again? Even today, that could be in the region of fifteen hundred million! No stadium on earth could hold such a number. Even the whole city of Jerusalem would be far too small.

14

The Bible gives a twofold answer.

First, it will take place *outside* the city. Jesus ascended to heaven from the Mount of Olives, a peak to the east with a panorama of the whole city on one side and the wilderness down to the Dead Sea on the other. It was on the slopes of this mountain that thousands of pilgrims to the three annual Jewish feasts used to camp, and it was here that they welcomed Jesus with palm branches when he rode into Jerusalem on a donkey (Mark 11:8-10). The same prophet who predicted that event (Zechariah 9:9) also foretold: *'On that day his feet will stand on the Mount of Olives'* (Zechariah 14:4). Jesus is returning to the very same spot he left. Yet the mountain can hardly hold the millions on this occasion.

Second, it will all take place *above* the mountain! We *'will be caught up... in the clouds to meet the Lord in the air'* (1 Thessalonians 4:17). There is certainly plenty of room in the sky, but how will the law of gravity be overcome? By then we shall have received our new 'immortal' bodies (1 Corinthians 15:51-53), just like his 'glorious' body (Philippians 3:21), which was equally at home on earth or in heaven, able to eat fish and cook breakfast yet pass through locked doors and step into space without a space-suit!

Imagine this vast multitude floating among the clouds. Few elements in God's creation give us a clearer picture of his glory. Those who have flown above cumulus clouds bathed in radiant sunshine will understand. The sight is 'glorious'.

It means that the wind will be westerly on that day, bringing moisture from the Mediterranean. East winds from the Arabian desert bring only dry scorching heat. This was how God blessed or punished his people Israel (1 Kings 17:1; 18:44). The return of their Messiah will be the greatest blessing they ever received.

How?

This aspect of his return is best approached by comparing it with his ascension and contrasting it with his advent. His second coming will be like his first going, but unlike his first coming.

It was the angels who first drew the parallel between his

ascension and his return: *'This same Jesus... will come back in **the same way** you have seen him go into heaven'* (Acts 1:11).

In other words, had one of the disciples had a camcorder and made a video of his departure and disappearance, this could have been used to portray his return, just by showing it backwards! The one event is simply the reverse of the other. They belong together, though one is past and the other future.

Some contemporary scholars dismiss the ascension as a myth, as fiction rather than fact, as conveying theological truth about who Jesus was but not historical truth about where he went. They regard themselves as too sophisticated to accept the idea that heaven is 'up there'. Not surprisingly, this creates real problems for thinking about his return. Most of them just don't!

Who do we believe, the angels or the scholars? Will Jesus come down from a cloudy sky in the same way in which he was taken up? Or is the whole thing a fairy-tale? The choice is yours!

Those who accept the eye-witness testimony of those who saw him go have no difficulty believing that he will come back in the same manner. His return will be visible, audible and tangible.

However, while his part in the picture will be the same, other aspects will be quite different.

There were only two angels attending his ascension but thousands will accompany his return (Matthew 25:31; Jude 14). Only eleven men saw him go but millions will see him come back. The whole scene will be crowded.

And there will be more to hear as well as see. One statement about his return has been described as 'the noisiest verse in the Bible' (1 Thessalonians 4:16). God is speaking, the archangel is shouting, the trumpet is sounding – and it is difficult to imagine the millions watching remaining silent when for the first time they see the one whom they have loved for so long.

All this is in sharp contrast to his first coming. For his first nine months on earth he was completely invisible, hidden in the darkness of Mary's womb. Only a few close relatives knew of his presence. His birth was relatively unnoticed, except by a few shepherds, until wise men from the east (probably descendants of the many Jews who stayed in Babylon after the exile) alerted Herod to a potential rival. There were, of course, angels to announce his first advent as they would his second; and there was the star, one pin-point of light in the sky, whose significance was only realised by those looking for it. The 'king of the Jews' was only born in David's royal city, Bethlehem, because a distant emperor introduced a new poll tax. Even then, his cradle was an animal feeding trough.

It is obvious that the world was totally unaware of what was happening or of who had come. It was as if God himself wanted as little publicity as possible for his Son's intervention in history. This was to be a hidden visit to planet earth seen only by the eye of faith.

His second coming could not be more different; no longer as a helpless baby, but as a mature man; not with a single star in the sky, but with lightning from the eastern horizon to the west (Matthew 24:27); not in weakness but in power; not in humility, but in glory; not in meekness, but in majesty.

There will be universal awareness and instant recognition. Everyone will know he has come and everyone will know who he is. It will be the most public and publicised event in history.

New Testament writers searched the Greek language for words to describe this unique occasion. They settled on three, each of which had special associations, both in the Greek translation of the Hebrew scriptures and in the general usage of contemporary society.

'Parousia' was their favourite. It means 'to be beside' and was used generally when someone 'arrived' to join others who expected them. However, there were two particular applications which made it peculiarly appropriate for the second coming, both connected with royalty. One was when a foreign king 'arrived' with his army at the border of a land he intended to invade, conquer and occupy. The other was when a native king 'arrived' with his court to visit one of his cities; in this case, the leading citizens would go out to meet him well outside the city wall, so that they might honour him by processing through the gates with him. These two images perfectly combine the dual aspect of Jesus' return. Unbelievers will see him as an alien invader; believers will welcome and honour him as their sovereign.

'Epiphaneia' can best be translated as 'appearing on the scene',

17

with the hint of a sudden rather than a gradual coming into view. Again, it has been used of an invading army or a king visiting his subjects – much as the British royal family 'appears' on the balcony of Buckingham Palace before the assembled crowd below. Its highest use is in the context of worship, when God manifests himself in visual ways – as when the 'Shekinah' glory came down on the Tabernacle or Temple. This last application often carried the nuance of bringing comfort and support. God was appearing on the scene to help his people, especially at a critical time of need. This meaning may be illustrated by 'Western' films, when the cavalry troops come over the horizon in the nick of time to *save* the pioneer settlers from Red Indian attack. That is an 'epiphany', and explains why the word is used of the first as well as the second coming of Jesus.

'*Apokalypsis*' takes the notion of 'arriving' and 'appearing' one step further. The root of the word is to hide but the prefix changes the meaning to uncover what has been hidden. Applied to persons, it means to unveil. The English colloquialism: 'to be shown up in one's true colours' is an excellent equivalent. Applied to royalty, it would mean wearing the crown, robes and jewellery befitting a sovereign. It is to be fully revealed as one is for all to see. For obvious reasons, this could not be used of Jesus' first coming, but is entirely appropriate for his second, when he comes '*with power and great glory*' (Matthew 24:30).

There is a children's story in which an Emperor, disguised as a beggar, mingles with his people the day before an intended visit, to see how they will treat him as a person; the following day is his '*apokalypsis*', with full regalia and retinue, causing great shame and embarrassment as the 'beggar' is recognised as supreme ruler. So it will be when Jesus appears as King of kings and Lord of lords. Significantly, the book of Revelation, which says more about his coming than any other, begins with the words '*The apokalypsis of Jesus Christ...*' (Revelation 1:1). It is one of a number of 'apocalyptic' books in the Bible which 'uncover' the hidden future (Daniel and Ezekiel are examples).

These three words together provide a vivid description of this unique event. It is important to note that they are used interchangeably to indicate different aspects of the same occasion and not separate stages of an extended sequence, as some have mistakenly thought.

The common verb that ties them all together is 'come'. Jesus is coming. He is coming as a conquering king. He is coming to save his people.

He is coming as he really is. The world last saw him crucified; now it will see him crowned. At last every knee will bow and *'every tongue confess that Jesus Christ is Lord, to the glory of God the Father'* (Philippians 2:10-11).

But when will he come? How much longer do we have to wait?

When?

If we knew the answer to this, we would be possessors of the greatest secret in the world. No-one knows – except God himself. Even Jesus, when he was on earth, confessed ignorance of this date on his Father's calendar (Matthew 24:36). And he told his disciples they would not be able to find it out (Mark 13:33-35; cf. Acts 1:7). It seems important that we should *not* know (paradoxically, as we shall see, we are more likely to be ready if we don't know than if we do).

So is that all there is to be be said? Or can we still ask further questions?

Will his coming be sudden, totally unexpected? Or will there be indications of his impending return? To put it another way, will it be a complete interruption of the historical process or the climax of a series of preceding events? If we can't have the exact date, can we work out an approximate one? Quite simply, will we have any warning of his approach?

To this last, the New Testament appears to give two contradictory answers: yes and no!

On the one hand, in addition to the passages emphasising ignorance there are a number picturing his coming as a *'thief in the night'*, unexpected and unnoticed (Matthew 24:43; 1 Thessalonians 5:2; Revelations 16:15); there is a well-known Christian film with this very title. Since the essence of successful burglary is surprise, the implication is that there will be no warning of his coming, nor even any indication that he is near. Which means that Jesus can come back at 'any moment' (a phrase now used as a label for this view).

On the other hand, other passages speak of events preceding his return, things that have to happen first which are *'signs'* (or signals) announcing that he is *'at the door'* (Matthew 24:33), about to step through on to the stage of history again. Consistent with this are frequent exhortations to *'watch'*, as well as *'pray'* for his return. This cannot mean living with eyes glued to the clouds in the sky! Apart from the inherent danger, he will only appear above Jerusalem. The context is always one of world events, presaging the end of the age. In fact, the disciples asked Jesus *what would be the signs of his coming* (Matthew 24:3); and he gave them specific details in his reply. The practical implication of this is that he cannot (or will not) return until we *'see all these things'* (Matthew 24:33). We cannot therefore expect him 'at any moment', or even in the immediate future – though every generation of believers can validly hope it will be within their lifetime.

There is obviously a tension between these two strands of scripture. Bible students have resolved it in different ways. We shall look at three, two of which are questionable.

Some settle the issue by opting for one and ignoring the other. They either take the 'Any Moment' position or the 'Looking for Signs' approach. But building doctrine on only part of what the Bible says on a given subject leads to imbalance and extremism, with unfortunate practical results.

A more popular solution, particularly in America, is to assume that there are *two* second comings, separated in time. Jesus is coming twice, the first time secretly and unexpectedly for his bride the Church, the second publicly and with preceding signs to establish his Kingdom. This theory is relatively recent (it first gained popularity around 1830) and has been widely accepted. This view teaches that believers will be 'raptured' out of the earthly scene before they can 'watch' for the signs of his coming.

There is a much simpler and more scriptural way of understanding the paradox. There will not be two comings, but there will be two groups of people at the one coming. To one it will be a total shock, to the other no surprise.

Jesus himself compared the day of his return with the days of Noah (Matthew 24:37-39). Then, the majority of mankind were feeding and breeding, totally unaware of the impending disaster which came without warning. Yet Noah and seven others were ready, knowing what was coming and knowing it could not happen until the ark was completed. The boat itself was a long-term 'sign', the gathering of animals and storage of food a short-term 'sign'. But those who ignored or disbelieved the signs were completely taken by surprise.

This dual response runs right through the New Testament passages. To **unbelievers** Jesus' arrival will be a total surprise, a dreadful shock. To them he will appear a a 'thief', to rob them of all they have lived for. It will happen as suddenly as painful contractions come on a pregnant woman and will be equally inescapable (1 Thessalonians 5:3). But the very next verse states that **believers** will not be surprised (1 Thessalonians 5:4). They will have kept their eyes open, seen the signs and will be expecting him. They will be like the householder who heard that a burglar was intending to visit his home and stayed awake, 'keeping watch' for every sign of his approach (Matthew 24:42-43). However, even believers are exhorted to be self-disciplined, alert sentries, lest they fall into the world's stupor and be caught out themselves (1 Thessalonians 5:6-9).

So what are the signs of his coming? What are we 'watching' for? What events should we particularly notice as we read the newspapers and watch the television?

Here we run into a problem. We have so much data, almost too much, but it is scattered throughout the New Testament – some in the Gospels (particularly the first three), more in the Epistles (particularly the two to the Thessalonians) and a great deal in the book of Revelation.

Where shall we start? How shall we fit it all together? It's like trying to complete a jigsaw puzzle without the guidance of a picture on the lid. What we need is a basic framework into which all the pieces can be fitted. Is there such an outline anywhere in the New Testament?

Many think it is provided by the book of Revelation, which appears to give a sequence of future events (pictured as seals, trumpets and bowls). But the order is very complicated and detailed examination reveals that it is not strictly chronological (past events are recapitulated and future events are anticipated at irregular intervals). Actually the book was never intended to be a blue-print of the future and to treat it as such misses the practical purpose behind every part of it – to encourage believers to be 'overcomers' in the coming crisis (Revelation 3:5 and 21:7 are the keys).

That is not to say there is no order in its predictions. In fact, the sequence becomes much clearer towards the end, when the bad news gives way to the good news. But in the middle chapters it is far from simple or clear – which explains why it has led to so many different 'charts' in the commentaries. If we accept that its primary aim is to help believers endure suffering rather than identifying signs, we are free to look elsewhere for help with the latter.

Thankfully, the disciples once asked Jesus the very question we are asking: 'What will be the sign of your coming and the end of the age?' Jesus' answer is in each of the 'Synoptic' (similar viewpoint) Gospels (Matthew 24, Mark 13 and Luke 21). Unfortunately, they asked another question at the same time – when would Jesus' prediction about the destruction of the Temple come true (presumably they thought it would be at the same time, little dreaming they would be at least nineteen centuries apart!)? Jesus answered both queries together, so that the events of A.D.70 are blended with the signs of his coming (which may not be altogether misleading, since the two events have quite a lot in common, the one foreshadowing the other).

Of the three versions Luke concentrates on the earlier event, Matthew on the later. It is in the latter that we find the clearest outline, a fourfold framework of future events signalling his return, into which all the other information can be inserted.

After identifying the four basic 'signs' in the sequence, Jesus adds to each a warning about its attendant peril and counsel about the disciples' proper response to that. So for each sign there is a description, a danger and a duty (readers can easily make their own chart, which will be an aid to the memory). There is special emphasis on the risk that each will bring – namely, the deception of believers, misleading them in both belief and behaviour.

SIGN 1: Disasters In The World (24:4-8)

Three are specifically mentioned: wars, earthquakes and famines. The list is not exhaustive. Many others are mentioned in Revelation – for example, polluted rivers and oceans, outsized hailstones. The *'four horseman of the apocalypse'* cover imperial expansion and its resultant bloodshed, famine, disease and death. Clearly, these disasters have both natural and political causes.

An exponential increase in such catastrophes quickly spreads alarm and insecurity. In such a mood people look for a 'saviour' to avert tragedy, a situation ripe for unscrupulous claimants who will delude others and even deceive themselves into thinking that they are 'Christ'. The danger is a rash of false 'messiahs'.

Disciples must protect themselves from such deception by not allowing panic to make them vulnerable. They can do this by understanding these painful calamities in the opposite way to the world's reaction, not death-pangs of the old but birth-pangs of the new, not the end of all good things but the beginning of much better things. The appropriate response is not alarm and anxiety, but a sense of anticipation.

This sign is clearly visible. There have been thirty-six international conflicts since World War II, to say nothing of civil disturbances. Earthquakes are apparently doubling in number every ten years. Famine is widespread in the 'third' underdeveloped world. How long this state of affairs will continue or how much worse it can get, we cannot guess. But it is the first major sign of his coming.

SIGN 2: Deserters In The Church (24:9-14)

The changes will be of degree rather than kind, but will be universal in scale. Again, three features are mentioned, which relate to each other.

First, opposition. Followers of Jesus will be hated by all nations, which will bring a corresponding increase in martyrdom. There are approximately two hundred and fifty political 'nations' in the world today. Christians are under pressure in all but about thirty,

23

and that number shrinks annually. Churches everywhere need to prepare their members for suffering and sacrifice. The first three chapters of Revelation provide a curriculum for such schooling; indeed, the whole book is designed as a manual for martyrdom and covers every crisis likely to be encountered by the faithful.

Second, reduction. Such pressures quickly reveal the difference between genuine and nominal Christians. Mere churchgoers give way. Their love cools as a result of moral compromise with an increasingly wicked world. They will turn away from the faith, betraying Christ and Christians.

Third, expansion. Paradoxically, a church purified under pressure becomes a preaching church. This is confirmed throughout history and is particularly true of China today. This third development will be the completion of the task of world evangelisation. Only then can history be wound up, mission completed.

During this phase the danger shifts from false messiahs to false prophets, who are much more likely to deceive believers since true prophets are a continuing ministry within the Church. Discernment will be needed. From the Old Testament we have some guidance about the content of false prophecies. They offer *'Peace, peace – when there is no peace'* (Jeremiah 6:14; 8:11). They reassure with false comfort when trouble looms. Their message could be summarised as 'Don't worry, it may never happen'. One current example is the teaching that all Christians will be taken out of the world before the 'Big Trouble' or 'Great Tribulation' begins (see Sign 3 below). This leaves many Christians unprepared for the trials and testings ahead, which some of their brethren are already suffering.

Another characteristic of false prophecy is to make light of the sin in God's people, as if those who are the 'elect', the chosen of God, are eternally secure no matter what their moral or spiritual condition and will not be required to face personal suffering. The cliché 'Once saved always saved', a phrase which never occurs in scripture, encourages this kind of thinking. Jesus makes it quite clear that this is not the case. *'He who stands firm to the end will be saved'* (Matthew 10:22). Apostasy, the public denial of Christ in word or deed forfeits future salvation. *'But whoever disowns me before men, I will disown him before my father in heaven'*

(Matthew 10:33). The Book of Revelation takes the same line. The 'overcomers' will inherit the new heaven and earth but the 'cowardly' will be thrown into the lake of fire (Revelation 21:7-8).

What proportion will fail to stand firm to the end? It is a sobering challenge to read Jesus' prediction that *'many'* will turn away from the faith and the love of *'most'* will grow cold. The defection will not be negligible.

Yet there is an ever greater crisis to come which could wipe out even the faithful remnant, were it not for the fact that God in his sovereign power will strictly limit its duration.

SIGN 3: Dictator In The Middle East (24:15-28)

The troubles that have always afflicted God's people will reach a climax in a short, sharp crisis known as *'the Great Tribulation'* (Revelation 7:14) or *'the Big Trouble'*.

Jesus said more about this penultimate sign than the other three, but in a less straightforward way. His words need careful examination.

He based his warning on a phrase used three times by the prophet Daniel in the sixth century before Christ: *'the abomination that causes desolation'* (Daniel 9:27; 11:31; 12:11). A careful study reveals that Daniel was referring to a human conqueror who, in the very city where God had been honoured would utter blasphemous words and commit obscene deeds provoking great mental and physical distress among God's people.

This prophecy was partially fulfilled by the Seleucid king of Syria, Antiochus IV Epiphanes (= 'Glorious', though behind his back he was called Epimanes = 'Crazy'). In a reign of terror over Jerusalem for three and a half years in the second century before Christ, he ordered the Jews to abandon the laws of God, set up a Greek altar to the god Zeus in the Temple, sacrificed pigs on it and filled the priests' rooms with prostitutes. His tyranny ended in a revolt led by the Maccabees family and he died insane.

Even Daniel realised that there would be another such, even worse, *'at the time of the end'* (Daniel 11:35, 40; 12:4, 9, 12, 13). Clearly Jesus, speaking after Antiochus, endorsed this second fulfilment as still future. And there are notable similarities.

It will be for the *same period*. While Jesus simply said the days of this despot would be *'cut short'*, the book of Revelation is more specific: 1260 days, 42 months or 3½ years (*'a time, times and half a time'* Revelation 12:14).

It will be in the *same place*. Jesus advises all living in Judea at that time to leave as quickly as possible, without even waiting to pack. They must not remain in the vicinity of this man. That this is sound advice was demonstrated by the fact that no Christians died when Jerusalem was destroyed in 70 A.D., though a million Jews perished; they had fled across the Jordan to Pella the moment the emperor Titus and his troops arrived. Titus was no Antiochus, however. Hopefully believers in and around Jerusalem at the end of time will be as ready to act promptly. They must pray it will not be on the Sabbath when there will be no available transport or in the cold of winter since they will have to sleep out. Pregnant women and nursing mothers will have a particularly hard time keeping up in the flight.

Other passages in the New Testament speak about this last dictator. John alone calls him *'the antichrist'* (1 John 2:18 note that in Greek 'anti' means 'instead of', a substitute rather than an antagonist), though this is the title by which most Christians identify him. Paul talks about this *'man of lawlessness'*, who *'opposes and exalts himself over everything that is called God or is worshipped and even sets himself up in God's temple, proclaiming himself to be God'*, but he is *'doomed to destruction'* (2 Thessalonians 2:3-4). The ultimate blasphemy!

Again, the book of Revelation gives us most information, particularly in chapter 13. Here he is described as a *'beast'*, as is his religious colleague and co-conspirator, *'the false prophet'*. Together they set up a totalitarian regime in which only those who submit to this authority, by being branded with their mark, are allowed to buy and sell food and goods. The mark will be a number (666); the full meaning will be obvious when the time comes, but 6 is the human number, always falling short of the divine perfection of 7.

Since the authority of this tyranny will be universal rather than just local (Revelation 13:7), the *'distress'* will be unprecedented.

26

Nothing like it will have been experienced before or will be experienced after, said Jesus. It will be the greatest pressure his followers have ever known, terribly fierce but mercifully brief.

However, the greater danger will be the same one of deception. Such conditions will produce a plethora of false prophets *and* false messiahs, as eager to take their pickings as vultures gather around the body of an animal that has been attacked. With supernatural displays of occult power they will try *'to deceive even the elect'*, mimicking the example of the antichrist and the false prophet (Revelation 13:3, 14-15).

There will be many rumours that Christ has returned and believers will be told where they can find him. They must not listen to these rumours. They will see the sign that he has come, wherever they are at the time (see Sign 4 below). Only those in Judea must travel, not to encounter Christ but to escape Antichrist. The rest must stay where they are, keeping their ears shut and their eyes open. They must watch and pray.

This whole extraordinary scenario may be difficult to imagine or believe. But we have Jesus' word for it: *'See, I have told you ahead of time'*. It is a question of trusting his foreknowledge and truthfulness. How kind and thoughtful of him to prepare us with such detailed information. Those who accept and act upon it will be kept safe when the storm breaks.

Before considering the final sign, there are two very important points to note at the end of the 'Trouble' or 'Great Tribulation'. First, *Christ has not come yet*. There are plenty of rumours that he has, but the truth is that he has not. Second, *Christians have not gone yet*. They are still on the earth, experiencing the wide distress (note "you" and "your" throughout these verses). The only ones who escape are those who are martyred, though this will be a *'great multitude'* (Revelation 6:9-11; 7:9-17; 11:7; 13:15; 20:4). Others will be safely hidden in deserted areas (Revelation 12:6, 14). The warning that all who worship the beast and accept his mark will be *'tormented with burning sulphur... for ever and ever'* is seen as a call *'for patient endurance and faithfulness on the part of the saints'* (Revelation 13:9-12) lest they share this fate.

But this crisis can be measured in days and will soon be over. There will be only one more 'sign' before the Lord returns.

SIGN 4: Darkness In The Sky (24:29-31)

This will follow *'immediately after the distress of those days'*. There will be no more delay. This means that those who live to see the third sign will have a very good idea about when Jesus will come back. This knowledge should encourage them to hold on during those terrible months.

The final sign will be unmistakable. All natural sources of light will be extinguished, leaving the whole sky black as ink. Whatever the time of day, it will be the darkest night. Sun, moon and stars will be shaken out of their orbits, no longer able to shine upon planet earth. Hebrew prophets foretold it (Isaiah 13:10; 34:4; Joel 2:31, quoted in Acts 2:20).

The sky has already reflected key events in the life of Christ. The brilliant star at his birth and the eclipsed sun at his death are foreshadowings of the cosmic welcome to his return.

The absence of natural lighting will make the supernatural 'lightning' all the more noticeable. The sky which was pitch-dark will be filled with brilliant light, the glory of the only begotten Son of God, glimpsed so briefly by three disciples on Mount Hermon (Mark 9:3; John 1:14; 2 Peter 1:16-17), now blazed around the globe and seen by all.

In a theatre, when the house lights are turned off it is a signal that the drama is about to begin. The excited audience knows it will not have to wait long before the curtain goes up on a brightly illuminated stage, often a crowd scene with the main actor centre front. So it will be on 'that day'.

The nations will see the *'lightning coming from the east and flashing to the west'* and they will see Jesus riding on the clouds (just how is not explained; will it be caught by television cameramen?). As full realisation of the significance of what is happening dawns on unbelievers, they will be overcome with grief. How wrong they have been! What opportunities they have wasted! Now they will be the ones to experience unprecedented distress.

Not so the believers who have waited so long for this day to arrive. They too will see the lightning, but they will also hear the sound of a trumpet, loud enough to wake the dead! The ancient ram's horn ('shofar' in Hebrew) was a call to the Lord's people to gather together; this will be the same. Angels will escort believers from all four corners of the earth; for many, their first trip to the Holy Land, for all, their first free flight! They will already have their new bodies, as will the dead believers who precede them to this meeting of all meetings.

It is generally known as 'the Rapture'. In modern English, the word has strong emotional overtones, which are not inappropriate. But the word is actually taken from the Latin *RAPTO, RAPTERE* (which means to be 'snatched up' and is used in the Latin translation of 1 Thessalonians 4:17: *'caught up with them to meet the Lord in the air'*). The same double meaning can be found in the synonym 'transported'.

Of course, as believers are transported to Israel, unbelievers will be left behind. As Jesus said, there will be two men working together in the same field, one taken, the other left; the same can happen to two women working together in the same kitchen (Matthew 24:40-41). Even families will be forever divided (Luke 12:51-53).

But the faithful followers of Jesus will be forever united, both with each other and with their Lord (1 Thessalonians 4:17). Wherever he is or will be, he has come back so that they can be with him and see his glory (John 14:3; 17:24).

Such are the 'signs of his coming' which Jesus gave to his disciples and, through them, to us. Their content and sequence are clear, as is the increasing speed and the decreasing duration of their appearance.

Jesus encouraged us to look for these signs of history and to interpret them correctly, just as others interpret the signs of nature. When the sap rises in the fig-tree and the buds burst into leaf, the advent of summer is signalled (Jesus is drawing a simple analogy from the natural world; there is no hint that he is speaking metaphorically of the national restoration of Israel to its own land and political independence, even though the Old Testament occasionally likens the nation to a fig tree, more usually a vine). The analogy is between the budding leaves and the four 'signs' he has been speaking about. *'Even so, when you see **all** these things* (i.e. up to and including the darkened sky), *you know that he* (or, it) *is near, right at the door'* (Matthew 24:33).

It is vital to realise that Jesus' purpose in giving this detailed forecast was not to argue dates, but to avoid dangers. His intention was practical application rather than intellectual speculation. Alas, history is full of examples of those who have 'guestimated' the actual date. Martin Luther calculated it would be 1636, John Wesley thought of 1874; both were wise enough to choose a year well ahead of their having to live with their mistakes! Not so William Miller, founder of the Seventh Day Adventists, who chose 1844 or Charles Russell, founder of the Jehovah's Witnesses, who chose 1914; both died shortly after their dates expired. Recently there has been a rash of proposals, many highlighting 1988 (as the fortieth year after the 'fig-tree' State of Israel blossomed).

From all that has been said so far, it is obvious that we do not know the year and cannot know at this stage, when only the more general 'signs' are clearly visible. It is also clear that it cannot be this year, next year or even for the next few years. The hope that it will be in our lifetime depends on the extraordinary acceleration in world events. The end could come more quickly than we think.

However, there is one more thing we can say about the timing of his coming. We may not know what year it will be, but we do know what time of year it will be! God wrote into Jewish ritual foreshadowings of his later redemptive work through Christ, especially into the annual calendar of feasts. The three major festivals, when the people gathered in Jerusalem, were 'signs' of the Messiah. The first was Passover (March/April in our diaries), when the lamb was killed at 3pm, followed a few days later by presenting the 'first-fruits' of the harvest – clearly fulfilled in the death and resurrection of Jesus. The second was Pentecost (May/June), to give thanks for the law given at Sinai 50 days after the first Passover, though it led to the death of 3000 rebels (Exodus 32:28) – clearly fulfilled in the giving of the Spirit seven weeks after Calvary, bringing life to 3000 penitents (Acts 2:41; cf. 2 Corinthians 3:6).

The third, 'Tabernacles' (September/October), is the 'great' feast when Jews recalled the provision of manna in the wilderness by living in temporary shelters, and celebrated the final ingathering of the harvest. Christians celebrate Passover and Pentecost (as Easter and Whit), though now on differently calculated dates. But consciously or unconsciously, they ignore Tabernacles, because they do not see any connection with Christ. There is much more than they realise.

Jesus was probably born during this feast. He may have been conceived on December 25th, but most know he was not born on that pagan midwinter celebration of the returning sun in the northern hemisphere. A little research into scripture reveals that he was born fifteen months after Zechariah was on duty in the temple in the fourth month (1 Chronicles 24:10; Luke 1:5, 26, 36). Tabernacles fell in the seventh month. Is this why John says: *'the Word became flesh and lived for a while* (the Greek is 'tabernacled') *among us'* (John 1:14)?

He certainly visited the feast. His sceptical brothers urged him to use the occasion, knowing that this was the very time of year when the Jews expected their Messiah to appear. His response is very revealing: *'The time for me has not yet come; for you any time is right'* (John 7:6). But he did go, privately. And he did make a public appearance on the last and greatest day, on which water was carried from the pool of Siloam to pour on the altar with prayers that the early and latter rains might come again (there is no rain, only dew, for the six summer months), ensuring the next harvest. In this context, Jesus' shouted message takes on profound meaning: *'If a man is thirsty, let him come to me and drink. Whoever believes in me, as the Scripture has said, streams of living water will flow from within him'* (John 7:37-38). This caused a lively debate about his identity. Ironically, the possibility that he was the Messiah was dismissed because he came from Nazareth, not Bethlehem! What self-restraint Jesus showed in remaining silent.

However, the real fulfilment of this feast in Christ is in his second advent, not his first. Just as he died at Passover, sent his Spirit at Pentecost, he will return at Tabernacles. Right on time. God's time.

Every Jew knows this. Their own prophets foretold it. Zechariah predicted that the nations will thereafter *'go up year after year to worship the King, the Lord Almighty, and to celebrate the Feast of Tabernacles'* (Zechariah 14:16). Every year at this time, Jews pray that Gentiles may attend the feast to greet the Messiah. If any further confirmation is needed, the fact that it is immediately preceded by the Feast of Trumpets should settle the matter (Leviticus 23:23-25; cf. Matthew 24:31; 1 Corinthians 15:52; 1 Thessalonians 4:16; Revelation 11:15).

On the eighth day of the feast, Jews hold a wedding ceremony and get 'married' to the Law (a scroll held by a rabbi under the canopy). On that day they begin again their annual reading of the Pentateuch, the five books of Moses. One day it will be the *'wedding of the Lamb'* (Revelation 19:7). That's just one of the reasons why Jesus is returning – for his bride.

We began this section by considering what the scripture means by describing the second coming as 'sudden'. We must end by looking at the word 'soon', applied to the same event. *'Yes, I am coming **soon**'* (Revelation 22:20). The simple question is: how soon is 'soon'?

At first sight, the word leaves an impression that it could be 'any moment now'. But words need to be seen in the context of the whole teaching of the New Testament on any subject.

Some of its writers clearly held the possibility that Jesus would return in their lifetime. *'**We** who are still alive and are left will be caught up'* (1 Thessalonians 4:17; note 'we', not 'they'). Paul certainly hoped it would be (2 Corinthians 5:2-3). He did not relish the disembodied state between death and resurrection, though he preferred it to being in his present body.

On the other hand, there are clear indications that they did not expect him back at any moment, that there would be a considerable lapse of time. The disciples had to take their testimony *'to the ends of the earth'* (Acts 1:8). Jesus predicted Peter's crucifixion in his old age (John 21:18), though in the same context he gave ground for a rumour that John would live until his return; John himself corrects this misunderstanding (John 21:23).

That generation, and the next, were disappointed. They had believed and preached that Jesus would 'soon' return as king. He had not. It became a topic for ridicule, even before the last page of the New Testament was written. Hecklers mocked the teachers: *'Where is this coming he promised? Ever since our fathers died everything goes on as it has since the beginning of creation'* (2 Peter 3:4).

The problem is even more acute for us, after fifty or more generations have come and gone. We may be much *nearer* the event, but such a long delay makes us wonder if we are anywhere *near* it. Does 'soon' make any sense to us today? Dare we use it confidently in our preaching? How do we cope with it?

Some scholars simply dismiss the word as a 'mistake'. They assert that Paul, and even Jesus himself, were wrong to use this word, even if they sincerely believed it. Though this explanation is widely accepted in liberal circles, it is untenable to those who believe the Bible to be the inspired word of God, who would not allow such a misleading error to be left for us to read.

The Bible is a self-interpreting book, one part explaining another. In fact, the same chapter in which the scoffing jibe about his delay is mentioned includes a two-fold answer to it.

First, *time is relative*. To the Greeks, God was outside time. To the Hebrews, time was inside God. Time is real to him (even he cannot change the past); but it is relative to him. It is also relative to us. (When Einstein was challenged to give a simple presentation of this theory of time's relativity, he replied: 'One minute sitting on a hot stove seems longer than one hour talking to a pretty girl'!) It is even more relative to God. *'But do not forget this one thing, dear friends: With the Lord a day is as a thousand years, and a thousand years a like a day'* (2 Peter 3:8; quoting Psalm 90:4). The day God left his beloved Son alone on the cross must have felt like a millennium, but it must seem only a couple of days since God had him back at his side again.

So we should take 'soon' with God's sense of time rather than ours. The second coming is the very next big event on his calendar, even if it isn't on ours. Just a day or two more, or perhaps even just a few 'hours', from heaven's point of view. Notice the constant use of 'day' and 'hour' in connection with this happening (Matthew 24:36; John 5:28; Revelation 14:7); this may also explain the *'silence in heaven for about half an hour'* (Revelation 8:1).

So 'the Lord is not slow in keeping his promise, as some understand slowness' (2 Peter 3:9). He only seems slow to us, who operate on a different time-scale and in an age of 'instant' products seek immediate solutions to tension. We have lost the art of waiting for anything, never mind waiting on the Lord. Yet even saints can get tired of waiting. One such read the verse: 'For in just a very little while, he who is coming will come and will not delay' (Hebrews 10:37) and cried out: 'But, O Lord, it is a very long little while!'

So why did the Lord leave the word 'soon' in the scripture, knowing it could be misunderstood (by giving it a human rather than a divine meaning), leading to disappointment and impatience? Actually it does more good than harm. Somehow the word stimulates frequent recall of this future crisis. Life is to be seen in this perspective. In a very real sense, his return is the next big event on our calendar as well as God's. 'Soon' reminds us to start getting ready now. For, as we shall see in the second part of this book, Jesus is not so concerned about what we are doing when he comes back as with what we have been doing all the time he has been away. We need to keep constantly in mind our accountability to him on that Day. The little word 'soon' does that very effectively.

Second, *delay is beneficial.* Instead of grumbling about it, we should be glad. It means that judgement is also postponed. It is an expression of God's reluctance to close the door of salvation quickly. *'He is patient with you, not wanting any to perish, but everyone to come to repentance'* (2 Peter 3:9). This same God waited over a century before sending the flood (Genesis 6:3; this was not a reduction in life span, since it was not the average age afterwards); indeed, he waited nearly a millennium, the lifetime of Methuselah, since his first announcement of that judgement to Enoch (Jude 14-15). Today this same God is patiently extending to us the opportunity to change our way of living before it is too late. Note how often Jesus drew a parallel between the days of Noah and the day of his return (Matthew 24:37), as did his disciples after him (2 Peter 3:5-6).

In other words, if delay makes Christians disappointed for themselves, they should be delighted for the sake of others! And they might ponder on the thought that had there not been a long delay, they themselves would never have known God's love and all that he *'has prepared for those who love him'* (1 Corinthians 2:5).

But we are human. Having *'tasted the goodness of God and the powers of the age to come'* (Hebrews 6:5), we naturally want the rest as soon as possible. To the promise of Jesus: *'Yes, I am coming soon'*, our instinctive and understandable reaction is to cry: *'Amen. Come, Lord Jesus'* (Revelation 22:20).

Why?

This is by far the most important question to ask about the second coming. Strangely, it is the most neglected!

Many Christians who rejoice in the fact of his return rarely think of its purpose. For them it is apparently enough to look forward to having him with them once again.

But why should this bring pleasurable anticipation when every believer can look forward to being with him in heaven immediately after death, *'away from the body and at home with the Lord'* (2 Corinthians 5:8)? Won't fellowship with him be sweeter outside the context of this sad, sick, sinful world?

Is it that they hope his return will come before their death, thus avoiding death (and burial or cremation) altogether? Certainly, no-one relishes being measured up to be put in a wooden box! Or is it that they somehow feel that fellowship with his physical presence is somehow more real and desirable than his 'spiritual' presence in heaven?

Let us suppose that he is not coming back to earth, that he will stay in heaven until all his people join him there, where they will live with him for ever (which is quite a common notion, both inside and outside the church). Ask yourself whether this would really affect your belief or, even more relevant, your behaviour. What is your honest answer?

So far we have been thinking subjectively about the effect on ourselves. Let us look at it more objectively, and the results for the world.

Why does he need to return? Why does the world need him back? What did he not do on his first visit that requires a second?

Did he not complete his mission? What will he yet do here on earth that he cannot do from his position of supreme authority in heaven?

To some, such questions are inappropriate, even impudent. They see such delving into the mysteries of divine sovereignty as mere speculation. They are content with the revealed fact of his coming, to 'wait and see' what he does when he comes. However, there are two reasons for going further than this.

First, scripture itself gives a number of clear reasons for his return and hints at others. We are at liberty to follow up all the clues. Second, the more we understand the purpose of his return, the more we can appreciate its central importance to our hope for the future and the more it will affect the way we live in the present (this last aspect will be explored in the next chapter).

To stimulate your thoughts, let me raise two further questions which Christians don't seem to consider very often.

How long will he stay? His first visit lasted a third of a century. Will his second be shorter or longer? Can what he has to do be done quickly or will it take quite a lot of time? Will there be another 'ascension' or will he remain here permanently?

Why do we have to come back? Not only is Christ returning to planet earth; all believers now in heaven are also returning. *'We believe God will bring with Jesus those who have fallen asleep in him'* (1 Thessalonians 44:14). Christians expect to live on this earth a second time! When did you last hear that preached at a funeral?

We are now ready to ask why Christ, and Christians, need to come back here. What objectives does the Lord have in mind?

To Complete The Saints

The first thing to grasp is that salvation is a continuing process, not an instantaneous change at conversion. It is not yet complete in any Christian, though it is more developed in some than others.

That is why the New Testament uses the verb 'save' in three tenses – we have been saved, we are being saved and we will be saved. This corresponds to the three phases known as justification, sanctification and glorification, which together constitute salvation.

The process will reach its goal when every part of our being is restored to its original condition, when God created us in his own image. We know what that will be like, for his Son is *'the exact representation of his being'* (Hebrews 1:3).

The transformation will be complete when he returns. *'We know that when he appears, we shall be like him, for we shall see him as he is'* (1 John 3:2). As he perfectly reflects his Father, we shall perfectly reflect him.

That is why scripture is able to say: *'He will appear a second time, not to bear sin, but to bring salvation to those who are waiting for him'* (Hebrews 9:28). At last, Christians will be fully 'saved', (then able to say with confidence 'once saved, always saved'!). Their Saviour will have completed his work *in* them, as on his first visit he completed his work *for* them, on the cross (*'It is finished'*; John 19:30). He will see the results of all his suffering and be satisfied (Isaiah 53:11).

We must be careful not to be too 'spiritual' when we think about 'full salvation'. Western Christians are prone to this distortion in a culture more influenced by Greek thinking than Hebrew, in which physical and spiritual are widely separated, morally as well as mentally. Perfection is defined in terms of a soul in heaven rather than a body on earth. Eastern mysticism has a similar contempt for the material world.

But the creation is basically good, because it came from the hand of the good Creator. He wanted a physical universe and intended human beings to have physical bodies. Though sinful rebellion (angelic and human) has ruined his creation, God intends to redeem it, by restoring its original state.

Salvation, therefore, means transforming every part of us, physical as well as spiritual. It is frustrating to be half saved, trying to live the new spiritual life in our old physical bodies (and brains) programmed over the years with wrong habits. The tension was well expressed by Paul: *'For in my inner being I delight in God's law; but I see another law at work in the members of my body'* (Romans 7:22-23).

Of course, death of the body brings some relief. But it is only a partial solution to the problem, for the person God intended is incomplete, *'unclothed'*, *'away from the body'* (2 Corinthians 5:4,

8). That may be enough for Greek philosophers and Oriental mystics, but it will never satisfy those who know what God is really like and what he really wants for them. *'We ourselves, who have the firstfruits of the Spirit, groan inwardly as we wait eagerly for our adoption as sons, the redemption of our bodies'* (Romans 8:23).

What a paradox! Because we have the Spirit, we long for new bodies! Like salvation, our 'adoption' as sons of God is future as well as past (cf. Romans 8:15). The crowning climax of our restoration will be the gift of a brand new body, uncontaminated by our sinful past, unlimited in its expression of the spirit within, unaffected by disease, decay or death. Unlike the old, this new body will develop instantaneously, *'in a flash, in the twinkling of an eye'* (1 Corinthians 15:52). What will the evolutionist make of that?!

It will happen the moment the last trumpet sounds to herald the coming of Christ. His return and our resurrection will be simultaneous. The promise that *'we shall be like him, for we shall see him as he is'* (1 John 3:2) covers the whole of us – body, soul and spirit. Our new bodies will be *'like his glorious body'* (Philippians 3:21). Does that not mean that we shall be neither very young nor very old but, like him, in the very prime of life?

But why do we have to come back to earth to experience this metamorphosis of our flesh? Why could we not receive our new bodies in heaven? For that matter, why do we have to wait until we receive new bodies together, all at once? Why not at the moment each of us dies?

The answer is really quite simple: we don't need bodies in heaven, but we do on earth. Heaven is a place for spirit-beings. *'God is Spirit'* (John 4:24). The angels surrounding his throne are *'ministering spirits'* (Hebrews 1:14). The *'heavenly Jerusalem'* is crowded with *'the spirits of righteous men'* (Hebrews 12:23).

However, when heavenly beings come to earth they need bodies. The Son of God had to be incarnate – *'a body you prepared for me'* (Hebrews 10:5). Angels have to assume human form (Genesis 18:2; 19:1; cf. Hebrews 13:2). Even the fallen angels we call demons inhabit the bodies of others, human or animal (Mark 5:12-13). To operate in this physical world, a physical body is needed.

The implications are profound. If the 'saints' of all ages receive new bodies down here, that surely indicates that they are being fitted for continued life on earth rather than in heaven. It begins to look as if both Christ and Christians come back to stay, to remain on this planet. That would mean that believers still living on earth when Jesus returns will never go to heaven! Even those who went to heaven when they died were in temporary accommodation!

The Bible clearly depicts 'earth' as the ultimate destiny of all who have been saved. But not this old earth, a new earth. The same almighty power of God redeeming our bodies will also redeem our environment. There will be a new earth for our new bodies to live in (we shall consider this later, as well as the question about how quickly this will come after Jesus returns).

We know that our salvation will be complete when Jesus returns, but God's saving purpose will not be fulfilled until the entire universe has been restored to its original condition.

As well as the individual and universal aspects of God's plans for our world, there is to be one national restoration.

To Convert The Jews

Jesus was and is Jewish. He was born and died as *'King of the Jews'* (Matthew 2:2; 27:37). He *'was sent only to the house of Israel'* (Matthew 15:24). Almost his entire ministry was spent in his own land and among his own people. It is true that most of them did not receive him (John 1:11), but from those who did we have received the Bible (all but one of its forty authors were Jewish) and the Church (all the twelve apostles and most of the initial members were Jewish).

Many Christians seem to have forgotten that their Saviour is a Jew and *'salvation is from the Jews'* (John 4:22). The Church seems to have pulled up its Jewish roots (for example, in moving Easter, Whitsuntide and Christmas away from the dates for Passover, Pentecost and Tabernacles). Worse than that, Christians have set the pace for anti-semitism throughout Church history, notoriously in the Crusades. Jews have suffered more in 'Christian' countries than any other, right up to the 'holocaust' in Germany. Behind this attitude lie two gross errors.

First, **that the Jews killed Jesus**. The entire nation, past and present, is held to be guilty of deicide (the murder of God). How can the Jews of today be held responsible, even though they still refuse to recognise Jesus as the Son of God? Even more Gentiles do the same. Are contemporary Christians ready to be found guilty for the Crusades? Even in Jesus' day, the whole nation was not involved in the crucifixion. 'The Jews' in John's Gospel are the inhabitants of Judea, southerners, not Galileans. Jesus made it clear that Gentiles would be his actual executioners (Matthew 20:19, March 10:33; Luke 18:32). And in a sense we are all responsible for his death, since he was suffering for the sins of the entire human race.

Second, **that the Church replaced Israel**. Since the Jews rejected their Messiah, Gentiles who accept him claim to constitute the 'new Israel'. God's covenant purposes have been totally transferred from one people to another. Jews have virtually become Gentiles, just one of the many nations of the world, outsiders to the kingdom of God. God's plans for the future do not include the Jewish people as such. So it is said.

Certainly this seems to be implied by some statements of Jesus (Mark 21:43) and Paul (Acts 13:46; 15:17; 28:28; Romans 9:24-26). Many of the Old Testament descriptions of Israel are given to the Church in the New (1 Peter 2:9-10); the same applies to some of the promises made to them (Hebrews 13:5-6). But that is not the whole story.

God's covenant with Abraham and his descendants was 'everlasting' and therefore unconditional (Genesis 17:7). To remove all doubt, God later spelled out what this would mean: *'I will not reject them or abhor them so as to destroy them completely, breaking my covenant with them. I am the Lord their God'* (Leviticus 26:44; cf. Deuteronomy 4:31; 9:5-6; 2 Samuel 7:15; Psalms 89:34; 94:14; 105:8-9; 106:45; 111:5; Amos 9:8; Jeremiah 30:11; 14:21; Ezekiel 16:60; 20:44; Malachi 3:6). Though he would scatter them among the nations when they broke their part of the covenant, God would never break his and would bring them back *'from the four corners of the earth'* (Deuteronomy 32:26; Isaiah 11:12). Such a worldwide dispersion and return did not happen in the Babylonian exile, but is happening today. It was to a people restored to their land that he promised a deliverer from Zion, a new covenant and his outpoured Spirit (Isaiah 59:20-21; Jeremiah 31:1-40; Joel 2:28-32). Despite all attempts to annihilate them, these people have survived physically and a 'remnant' of them have remained spiritually faithful to their God (1 Kings 19:18).

The New Testament endorses all of this. God is still the *'God of Abraham, and the God of Isaac, and the God of Jacob'* for they are still alive (Luke 20:37-38). The name 'Israel' is mentioned over seventy times. It is always applied to Abraham's physical descendants with one doubtful exception (Galatians 6:16, if the Greek word *KAI* is translated 'even', instead of its normal meaning 'and' as in the New English Bible).

Jesus foresaw both the immediate rejection by his fellow-countrymen and their ultimate restoration. Even while weeping over Jerusalem's refusal to accept his protection, he predicted: *'You will not see me again **until** you say: Blessed is he who comes in the name of the Lord'* (Matthew 23:39; significantly, this is one of the 'Hallel' or 'Praise' psalms 113-118, sung at the Feast of Tabernacles). He anticipated the fall of Jerusalem in A.D. 70, but that it would only be *'trampled on by the Gentiles **until** the times of the Gentiles are fulfilled'* (Luke 21:24). The disciples' last question to him before his ascension concerned the timing of the restoration of the monarchy to Israel. Instead of rebuking the irrelevance of their thinking (as many Christians would today), he told them that the date already fixed by his Father was not of immediate concern to them – they had a mission to be his witnesses to the ends of the earth, the Gentile nations (Acts 1:6-8). He had already told them they would one day govern the courts of the twelve tribes (Matthew 19:28; Luke 22:30), but this would have to wait. The one thing certain is that *'this race will certainly not pass away **until** all these things have happened'* (Matthew 24:34 NIV margin; 'these things' are the signs of his coming).

In a passage specifically dealing with the future of the Jewish race (Romans 9-11), Paul clearly teaches that God has not rejected them, even though they have rejected him (11:1). He acknowledges that not all Abraham's physical descendants are his spiritual children sharing his faith (9:6-7; cf. 2:28-29). So many Jews are not 'saved' and need to believe in Jesus (10:1). Paul, with a similar

41

anguish over his people as Moses, would willingly go to hell if it would get them to heaven (Romans 9:3; cf. Exodus 32:32).

Nevertheless, Israel cannot *'fall beyond recovery'* (11:11), because *'God's gifts and his call* (to the patriarchs) *are irrevocable'* (Romans 11:29). There has always been a 'remnant' and there always will be (11:6). Only 'some' of the branches of the 'olive tree' Israel, have been broken off and replaced by grafted 'unnatural' wild olive Gentiles (11:17, 24). These hybrid believers (i.e. Christians) need to remember that they too, are in danger of being 'cut off' if they do not continue to trust in the divine kindness (11:22). And they (i.e. the Jews) can be grafted back in our place, if and when they believe in Jesus, their Messiah, fitting into their own roots much more naturally (11:23-24). Indeed, there has been a Jewish minority in the Church of Jesus for two millennia and it is currently expanding.

But there is more. Paul made a startling prediction, which he called a 'mystery' (11:25). The scriptural meaning is: a former secret God has now revealed. The hardening of Jewish hearts against the Gospel, which is God's punishment for rejecting his redemptive initiative (as it was for Pharaoh; 9:17-18), is only partial and temporary *until* (that word again!) the full number of the Gentiles has 'come in'. Then it will be removed, the veil lifted from their minds (2 Corinthians 3:5-6), and *'so **all Israel** will be saved'*. This phrase does not include all Jews who have ever lived or even necessarily all Jews still alive at the end. The phrase 'all Israel' is frequently used in the old Testament of a representative national gathering from all the tribes of Israel, usually in Jerusalem (1 Chronicles 11:1; cf. Deuteronomy 1:1); it is perhaps best translated: *'Israel as a whole'*.

Since 'saved' must have the same meaning here as elsewhere (cf. 10:1), this prediction is nothing less than a mass conversion to faith in Jesus of the most resistant people on earth! How could such a thing happen? The answer is obvious: in the same way that it happened on the Damascus road to Saul, the persecutor of the Christians, who became Paul, the preacher of the Gospel. The posthumous appearance of Jesus of Nazareth is enough proof for any Jew that he is the Messiah.

This is precisely what will happen when Jesus returns to

Jerusalem. The same prophet who predicted his first coming on a donkey, and his second at the Feast of Tabernacles proclaimed this word of the Lord: *'And I will pour out on the house of David and the inhabitants of Jerusalem a spirit of grace and supplication. They will look on me, **the one they have pierced**, and mourn for him as one mourns for an only child, and grieve bitterly for him as one grieves for a firstborn son'* (Zechariah 12:10; cf. Psalm 22:16: *'They have pierced my hands and my feet'*). The same word is taken up in the book of Revelation: *'Look, he is coming with the clouds, and every eye will see him, even those who **pierced** him'* (Revelation 1:7). One can hardly imagine their anguish over the unnecessary suffering and wasted opportunity of two thousand years – but it will not leave them in hopeless despair. As their fathers looked to a brass serpent on a pole for healing, they will now look to the Son of man and be saved (Numbers 21:8; John 3:14-15). What a welcome they will give him as he enters the city again (Matthew 23:39).

There are two important implications of this amazing result of Jesus's return.

The first is that the Jews will have been preserved as a people and restored to their land and capital. This has already happened. Many Christians rightly see this as a necessary prelude to the Lord's coming, but wrongly use it as an indicator of an imminent return. As we have seen, this immigration was not specifically included by Jesus in *'the signs of the times'*.

Furthermore, it means that Jerusalem will remain in Jewish hands in spite of predicted international assaults (e.g. Zechariah 12:1-3) and that a representative portion of the people will be supernaturally protected through all their troubles, including the 'Great Tribulation'. This surely is the meaning of the 'sealing' of the 144,000 from all the tribes of Israel (Revelation 7:1-8).

The second is that the future destiny of the Jews and the Gentiles who believe in Jesus is identical. Both come into the same salvation through the same Saviour. Jesus, speaking to Jews about Gentiles, said: *'I have other sheep that are not of this sheep-pen. I must bring them also. They too will listen to my voice, and there shall be one flock and one shepherd'* (John 10:16).

There is a common misconception that Jews have an earthly

destination and Christians a heavenly one. The Bible clearly teaches that they will live together in the new heaven and new earth, in a new Jerusalem that has the names of the twelve tribes of Israel on its gates and the names of the twelve apostles of Jesus on its wall foundations. They will be one people living under one (new) covenant.

To Conquer The Devil

Evil is not an abstract object with an independent existence. That means that the question 'why did God create evil?' is really meaningless. There is no such thing.

Evil is personal, not impersonal, an adjective, not a noun. It describes creatures who rebel against their Creator and do things their way rather than his. God did create beings, both on earth, and in heaven, who were capable of becoming 'evil' by their own free choice. This resulted in evil angels and evil humans, apparently in that order (Genesis 3:1). Between them they are responsible for all the 'evils' in nature and history. Such is the biblical diagnosis.

The leader of the heavenly rebellion was the fallen angel we call the devil, known by many names and titles – Satan, Beelzebub; serpent, dragon, lion, murderer, liar, destroyer. He persuaded many fellow angels to join his bid for a rival kingdom to God's (Revelation 12:4 indicates a third of the angels). We know them as demons.

Both the devil and his demons are given titles of authority and influence in Scripture. He is the ruler, prince and even 'god' of this world. They are principalities and powers. With the superior strength, intelligence and ability of angels they are able to wreak havoc in the affairs of men. They can manipulate us through disease in the body and deception in the mind. Their most potent weapon is death and the fear it brings (Hebrews 2:15). They can divide us from God and one another – and have done so since the garden of Eden. Their successful bid for power has been even greater on earth than in heaven: *we know... that the whole world is under the control of the evil one*' (1 John 5:19).

However, the devil is not God, though he would like to be and may even think he is. He is not omniscient (he doesn't know everything and can make blunders, one of which was to persuade Judas to betray Jesus; John 13:27). He is not omnipresent (he can only be in one place at once, which many Christians seem to forget; Job 1:7; Luke 4:13). He is not omnipotent; his power is strictly limited, in two ways:

First, he is no match for God. From the beginning until now, he can only act by God's permission (Job 1:12). God is still in complete control. Satan is no problem to him, though he is to us. This, of course means that God allowed him to take over our world. We can see both divine justice and mercy in this, justice because those who refuse to live under the rule of a good king deserve a bad one, mercy because that increases the incentive to desire the original regime.

Second, he was no match for Christ. Jesus began and ended his public mission by confronting the devil on his own territory – and successfully resisting his subtle and seductive temptations. For the first time in history an entire life was lived in freedom from his clutches, breaking his monopoly hold on the human race (John 12:31; 14:30). The cross was a fatal blow to his power, a triumph over the principalities and powers (Colossians 2:15). Through Jesus' atoning death and interceding life, it is now possible for men and women to live in freedom from the force of evil and their fear of death (Luke 22:31; Hebrews 2:14 -15).

But the final victory is not yet complete. There are now two kingdoms on earth – of God and Satan, good and evil, light and darkness. They are both growing, quantitively and qualitively, side by side (Matthew 13:30).

Why the overlap? Why didn't Satan's kingdom end when God's kingdom was re-established? A moment's thought will bring the explanation. If Christ had destroyed Satan and his followers as well as defeating them, the earth would have been uninhabited! God so loved Satan's victims that he wanted to give them every possible opportunity to transfer back to his rule, a liberation made possible through his Son (Colossians 1:13). Millions have now seized the opportunity. Alas, many more have not realised the door is open or have refused to go through it.

One day it will be shut. The kingdoms will not continue

together. The wheat and the tares will be separated at the time of harvest (remember the Feast of Tabernacles?). The poisonous weeds will be burned. A good God cannot allow evil to continue spoiling things for ever. He must call a halt sometime.

So Satan's days are numbered. His doom is decided and dated. When Jesus returns, Satan must leave. The world will finally be rid of him, having suffered his evil tyranny since the very first human beings walked the earth. Human history is proof of his existence and testimony to his character.

Since he knows his fate is sealed, we can expect his frustration to become more apparent as the end approaches (Revelation 12:12). He will put all his resources into a final bid to regain his dominion. Fortunately, *'we are not unaware of his schemes'* (2 Corinthians 2:11). With the promise of *'peace and security'* (1 Thessalonians 5:3), he will set up one world government with one world religion. In charge of each will be two men who will accept his offer of status and power (once refused by Jesus! Luke 4:5-8). They will be puppets under the devil's authority.

We have already mentioned this 'unholy trinity' (Satan, antichrist and the false prophet are a dreadful counterpart of God, Christ and Holy Spirit). They will together rule the world as never before in the last few years before Jesus returns. No wonder it is called the 'Big Trouble' or 'Great Tribulation'.

But this last fling of the devil will still be under God's over-ruling control and be kept mercifully brief.

Their final joint act of defiance will be to gather an international military force intent on slaughtering the apparently defenceless people of God, now gathered in Jerusalem with their returned Lord, Jesus. This will be the last battle in a history of continuous warfare. Scripture locates it in the plain of Esdraelon, the valley of Jezreel, near the ancient fortress town of Solomon on the small 'hill of Megiddo' (in Hebrew, 'Harmageddon'); Winston Churchill called this site of so many fierce actions: 'the cockpit of the Middle East'. The roads from Europe to Arabia and from Asia to Africa cross here.

It will be the devil's biggest blunder. The most basic tactical error is to under-estimate the strength of one's opponent. Jesus will come fully prepared for the conflict. No longer riding to

46

Jerusalem on a donkey as a symbol of peace, he will come on a horse as a symbol of war (Zechariah 9:9-10; Revelation 19:11).

Jesus will only use, only need to use, one weapon – the sword of his mouth (Revelation 19:15-21). It will be the same voice that commanded the wind and the waves to be still (Mark 4:39; the verb 'died down' comes from a root meaning to be smitten, cut off). Now a whole army will be slain – with a word! A field of corpses will be left unburied and provide a feast for vultures (Revelation 19:17, 21), the final humiliation for this rebel force.

But the two human 'beasts' behind it will not be killed. They will be taken prisoner and immediately *'thrown alive into the fiery lake of burning sulphur'* (Revelation 19:20). They will be the first two human beings to be sent to hell, even before the day of judgement, too depraved to be allowed to stand trial.

Surprisingly, the devil is not sent with them – not yet. He will be. But God has plans to use him just once more before he is sent to join his henchmen in everlasting torment (Revelation 20:10). Meanwhile, he is to be banished from the earth for a thousand years, kept in solitary confinement in the lowest dungeons of the underworld so that he can no longer communicate with and deceive the peoples on earth (Revelation 20:3).

So the world will at last be liberated from the devil and his oppressive forces of evil. It is difficult to imagine what that will mean for we have never known such a situation. We shall have to wait and see.

Will there be a world to see? Will it continue for a time or come to an end there and then? If it does go on, who will fill the political vacuum left by the collapse of the world government?

The Bible has yet another surprise for us.

To Command The World

Jesus told his followers to pray every day that God's kingdom, his rule, would *'come... on earth as it is in heaven'* (Matthew 5:10).

How and when will this prayer be answered?

Alas, Christians are deeply divided over this. The many different opinions may be grouped in three categories:

First, the pessimists. They believe this world is too far gone to be reclaimed. We can bring individuals into the kingdom (i.e. under God's rule). We can establish colonies of the kingdom (i.e. churches). But this world will remain in the devil's control and they will be destroyed together. Only in the 'new' earth will the kingdom be universally established. So this 'old' earth will 'pass away' immediately after the Lord returns. It will never know the blessings of being under God's government.

Second, the optimists. At the opposite end of the spectrum, they believe that the world will be 'Christianised' before Christ returns. This does not mean that everyone will be Christian, but that the church will grow and spread to be large and powerful enough to take over world government. This view also believes that this earth will end when he comes, since the kingdom will already have been established. In passing it may be noted that, on the present state and statistics of our world, the second coming must be a very long way off!

Third, the realists. Accepting Jesus' expectation that the kingdoms of God and Satan will *'grow together'* (Matthew 13:30), they anticipate increasing conflict between the two until the final confrontation between the returning Christ and the reigning antichrist. Of the outcome they have no doubt. Christ's victory over the forces of evil will clear the decks for his rule to be extended over the nations of the world. On this view, the 'old' earth will survive beyond his return, at least long enough for his reign to be demonstrated and appreciated.

Boiling down the debate to its simplest issue, we may propose the motion: that Jesus is coming back to this earth to reign over it. Not just to complete the saints, to convert the Jews and to conquer the devil – but to rule over the world for an extended period of time.

What does the New Testament say about this? The book of Revelation contains more information about the second coming than any other; so it is not surprising that the clearest indications of a reign of Christ after his return and on this earth may be found. Quite early on, there is a prediction that when the last trumpet sounds, the angels in heaven will sing and shout in celebration of a change of government: *'The kingdom of the world* (note the singular) *has become the kingdom of our Lord and of his Christ'* (Revelation 11:15).

However, it is at the end of the book, where the chronological order of events is very much clearer, that we find the fullest and clearest statement about a reign of Christ (20:1-10). We must take this passage in its context (chapters 19 and 21); chapter divisions, like verse numbers, are quite late and man-made, often putting asunder what God has joined together.

In its proper setting, this reign of Christ follows his return but precedes both the day of judgement and the creation of a new heaven and earth. Its location in time is therefore clear, as is its location in space. The action takes place on earth, not in heaven (20:1, 3, 8).

The duration of his reign on earth is even clearer. The phrase 'a thousand years' is emphatically repeated six times in this short passage, twice with the definite article: *'the thousand years'*. The Greek word is CHILIOI (from which we derive the label: 'chiliast', used of those who believe in this earthly reign of Christ); the Latin word is MILLENNIUM (source of the more familiar label: 'millennialist'). Those I have called 'pessimists', who don't believe Christ will *ever* take over the government of this world, are usually known as 'A-millennialist' (non-millennialist would be more easily understood). The 'optimists' are known as 'Post-millennialist', because they believe Christ will return *after* Christians have established a millennial rule on his behalf. The 'realists' are known as 'Pre-millennialist', because they expect Christ to return *before* his worldwide rule is actualised.

Whether the 'thousand years' are taken literally or symbolically, it is obviously a considerable period. Much can happen during it. What will the world be like when the devil is out of it and Jesus is in full control of political and natural events? Imagination is limited by the absence of any previous experience of such conditions; only Adam could tell us and his knowledge was severely restricted in time and space! Revelation is also limited. Scripture throws out many tantalising hints, but we may conclude that the Lord knows it would be unsettling for us to know more.

For example, the Hebrew prophets looked forward to the time when *'the earth will be filled with the knowledge of the glory of the Lord, as the waters cover the sea'* (Isaiah 11:9; Habakkuk

2:14); when every knee will bow to the Lord and every tongue confess his name (Isaiah 45:23, a prediction applied to Jesus in Philippians 2:10-11), when *'the Lord will be king over the whole earth'* (Zechariah 14:9).

They also foresaw some of the results of this just and benevolent reign; a time of unparalleled peace and prosperity would result from the settlement of international disputes by divine arbitration and multilateral disarmament; it is in this context that we find the memorable couplet: *'They shall beat their swords into ploughshares and their spears into pruning hooks'* (Isaiah 2:4; Micah 4:3) – words engraved in granite outside the United Nations headquarters in New York, but lacking any reference to the word of the Lord going out from Zion!

An abundance of food will be a source of health, in turn contributing to longevity. Death at one hundred years will seem a premature tragedy (Isaiah 65:20). There is an ancient Jewish notion that an ideal length of life on this planet would be one thousand years, based partly on the ages of their pre-flood fathers (none of whom quite made it, even Methuselah) and partly on the statement that *'a thousand years is like a day'* to God (Psalm 90:4; 2 Peter 3:8).

Even nature will reflect the change of government, with fertility in the vegetable world and harmony in the animal world: *'The wolf will live with the lamb, the leopard will lie down with the goat, the calf and the lion will feed together; and a little child will lead them. The cow will feed with the bear, their young will lie down together, and the lion will eat straw like the ox'* (Isaiah 11:6-7). Carnivores will become herbivores, as God originally intended (Genesis 1:30). Nature 'red in tooth and claw' was not his doing. The animals were never intended to be 'wild'. Children will safely play among them one day (Isaiah 11:8).

It is easy to dismiss all this as 'myth', as metaphysical fable rather than material fact. That is often a cover for our inability to imagine and therefore to believe in such a transformation. It is to question either the Creator's ability or his intention. If he once made a universe that was 'good' in every way, he *can* surely do it again. And if the purpose of redemption is to restore creation, he *will* surely do it again.

Let us return to the New Testament. Two aspects of the 'millennium' are specifically mentioned – one good news, the other bad news.

The good news is that believers, both Jews and Gentiles, will *reign on the earth'* with Christ (Revelation 5:10). Men *'from every tribe and language and people and nation'* (Revelation 5:9) will administer the government among their countrymen. Singled out for special honour will be those who successfully resisted the pressures of the last and worst totalitarian regime, even to the point of martyrdom (Revelation 20:4; note that this group is only one section of the company of those seated on 'thrones'). What a reversal! *'The meek will inherit the earth'* (Matthew 5:5).

This rule by the saints is frequently referred to in scripture – not just in Revelation (2:26 is another example) but in Daniel (7:18), in the Gospels (Matthew 19:28; 20:21-23; Luke 19:15-19) and in the Epistles (1 Corinthians 6:2; 2 Timothy 2:12). The prime qualification for responsibility then will be faithfulness now, trustworthiness as opposed to dishonesty, especially in such practical matters as money and property (Luke 16:10-12). Jesus will need many deputies to whom he can entrust key positions in his administration.

The bad news is that in spite of having the best government the world has ever seen and enjoying such ideal conditions, there will still be many who want to opt out of this kingdom of Christ. It is a lie that a perfect environment will produce perfect people, that prosperity brings contentment, that deep down everyone prefers peace to war. Human nature can only be changed from the inside, not the outside.

This sad fact will be amply proved at the very end of the millennium, in an extraordinary development. The devil will be released from his detention for one final opportunity to deceive the nations. He will find people wanting their 'freedom' from God and his people in every part of the globe. He will delude them into thinking that a military attack on the seat of government in Jerusalem will gain their political autonomy (has he not learned the lesson of Armegeddon or is this a suicidal act of defiance intended to take as many others with him as possible?). He will gather a huge army, perhaps the biggest ever, marching under the banner of 'Gog and Magog' (Revelation 20:8). There is a very detailed prophecy about this in Ezekiel 38-39 which places the event *after* the restoration of the Davidic monarchy in Israel (the names will become meaningful in the light of the event).

The attempt will be utterly futile. Fire from heaven will put an end to it and to all involved. Why should it have been allowed to happen at all?

The millennium can be considered from two perspectives as a finale to world history and as a prelude to the day of judgement. It will have conclusively demonstrated the sovereignty of God and the sin of man; his goodness and our badness – the two sides of historical reality that must finally be brought together to be eternally separated.

On the one hand, the world will have seen what life can be like under divine rule, when God acts as man has wanted him to act and constantly criticised him for not doing so, by forcefully removing evil powers from the earth. But what will happen when the human cry for liberation from suffering is heeded?

On the other hand, the world will be exposed as having no desire to be set free from the sin that has caused the suffering. There is still a race of rebels, still a mutinous desire for moral independence, still an ambition to be like gods (Genesis 3:5), to be landlords of the earth rather than its tenants.

The human race is without excuse. Given the very best opportunities and incentives, human beings still choose a godless existence which cannot remain neutral towards God or his people but must become hostile to both. The need for a day of judgement has been made abundantly apparent. The verdicts have been justified even before they have been announced. The stage is set.

To Condemn The Ungodly

Those whose beliefs are largely shaped by reciting creeds in church will be very familiar with this reason for his return. Both the 'Apostles' and the 'Nicene' creeds remind us that he will come to judge the quick (i.e. those still living) and the dead (already). Unfortunately they give the impression that this is the main, even the only, point of his second advent. As we have already seen, it is one of a number. Nevertheless, it is fundamental to his winding up of this 'present evil age', as the Jewish people called it.

It is necessary for history to conclude with a day of judgement. A little thought will reveal why.

The injustice of life demands it. It is so unfair that the wicked should prosper and the innocent suffer. Most crimes are undetected and unpunished. There seems to be little correlation between personal character and circumstance, integrity and prosperity, holiness and happiness. The universe appears to be based on blind chance – unless there is more to our existence than is bounded by cradle and grave. Instinct demands a time when good is rewarded and evil punished.

The justice of God demands it. If he never rights the wrongs he has permitted, his goodness is in question. If he is truly 'King of the universe', that position carries the responsibility of Judge as well. If it is true that: *'God cannot be mocked. A man reaps what he sows'* (Galatians 6:7), there *must* be a day of reckoning, when accounts are settled and bills paid in full.

But why a 'day' of judgement? Since death ends the opportunity and fixes a gulf between the good and the bad (Luke 16:26), why is each person not judged at that moment but kept waiting until the whole human race stands in the dock?

Because God must be publicly vindicated. He must be seen to be just in his decisions about our destiny. He has been so frequently accused of being unfair. These criticisms must be silenced, so that all will say, with Abraham: *'Will not the judge of all the earth do right?'* (Genesis 18:25).

Because Jesus must be publicly vindicated. His execution was the greatest injustice of all, the darkest day (quite literally) in human history. The last sight the world had of him was of a criminal in disgrace. All must witness the reversal of that verdict.

Because the Lord's people must be publicly vindicated. They made the right choice, took the side of God and right, yet in a wicked world paid the price for taking their stand, often with their lives. These, whom Jesus is not ashamed to call his 'brothers' (Hebrews 2:11; cf. Matthew 25:40), must be honoured in the presence of those who treated them with contempt and hatred.

There is, then, to be a 'day' when justice will be done. Every human being has two future engagements, neither of which can be entered in a diary or marked on a calendar. *'Man is destined to die once, and after that to face judgement'* (Hebrews 9:27). The first date is different for each; the second is the same for all.

Where will this great assize be held? There is a widespread impression that it will be up in heaven, perhaps due to the common but mistaken notion that everybody 'goes to heaven' when they die. Among Christians, there may be some confusion between *'the throne'* (in Revelation 4-5) and *'a great white throne'* (in Revelation 20:11; note the indefinite article), which are two different thrones, in two different places, occupied by two different persons. One is the throne of God in heaven and the other is the throne of Christ on earth.

Human beings will be judged on earth. This is where they have lived and where they have sinned. This is where their fate will be decided. How could a holy God allow sinners to enter heaven, even for a day?

Of course, many will have already died and will need to be brought back to life in order to stand trial. The Bible anticipates the resurrection of the wicked as well as the righteous (Daniel 12:2; John 5:29; Acts 24:15). Hades, the abode of departed spirits, will give up its inhabitants to be re-embodied. Everyone, whether buried, cremated or lost at sea will stand again on the earth, before their judge (Revelation 20:12-13).

Discerning readers will have already concluded that there will have to be *two* resurrection days, separated by the millennium. This is precisely what the New Testament teaches (Revelation 20:4-6). Actually, there are *three*, if the first Easter Sunday is counted (1 Corinthians 15:23-24; note the twofold 'then', indicating sequence).

Human beings will be judged on this earth – by a human being! This comes as a real surprise to those who expect God himself to be the judge. But he has delegated that function to one of us: *'For he has set a day when he will judge the world with justice by the man he has appointed'* (Acts 17:31). It is Jesus who will sit on the *'great white throne'* (Revelation 20:11; note the unidentified 'him'). *'For we must all appear before the judgement seat of*

Christ' (2 Corinthians 5:10).

During his life on earth, Jesus frequently claimed to have the authority to decide the eternal destiny of nations and individuals (Matthew 7:21-23; 13:41-43; 25:30-33). Such a claim can only be explained in one of three ways – that he was mad, bad or God; lunatic, liar or Lord. Only if he was the God-man, divine as well as human, is he perfectly qualified to be the Judge of all. And he has already done everything possible to save us from trial.

His dual nature enables him to apply perfect justice. His humanity gives him understanding. He has lived in our circumstances, under our pressures, with our temptations, without any advantages – yet without sin. His divinity gives him knowledge. He knows us through and through, our secret sins, our careless words, our hidden motives, our deepest emotions. His judgement will be absolutely just.

On the one hand, he will take into account our knowledge or ignorance of what is right and wrong in God's sight. The Bible makes it clear that we shall be judged according to the light we have received – whether the full light of the gospel, the half light of the ten commandments or the lesser light shining through creation outside and conscience inside (Romans 1:20; 2:12-16).

On the other hand, our entire life will be exposed, every thought, word and deed (Romans 2:6). Everything we have done while *'in the body'* (2 Corinthians 5:10). It has all been recorded in 'books', somewhat like the television programme volume: 'This is your life' except that God's account is exhaustive, not a selection of the commendable bits! These books will be opened on that day (Revelation 20:12).

What verdict can there be but: 'Guilty'? Who, confronted with such damning evidence, could argue with that verdict? Who has always done what they knew to be right, even if their only guide was their own conscience? Who has avoided everything they have criticised and condemned in others (Matthew 7:1)? Truly, *'there is no-one who* (consistently) *does good, not even one'* (Romans 3:12); *'all have sinned and fall short of the glory of God'* (Romans 3:23). None of us has been what God meant us to be or even what in our best moments we know we could and should have been.

The sentence is a living death in the place called hell, separated from God, the source of everything good, shut out of the new heaven and earth, shut in with the devil, demons and all who share their anger with their Creator, tormented, body and soul, day and night, for ever and ever in a *'lake of fire'* (Revelation 14:11; 20:10) with the anguish and frustration of knowing that wasted opportunities will never be repeated... no wonder Jesus spoke with horror of such a fate, warning his disciples of the danger and willing to sacrifice himself to save them from it. (Since this awesome subject is really beyond the scope of this booklet, readers are commended to the author's 'The Road to Hell', Hodder and Stoughton, 1992).

So is there no hope for anyone? Will the entire human race be condemned in that court? Look again at the scene. In addition to the millions of biographical volumes, *'another book was opened, which is the book of life'* (Revelation 20:12). Everyone listed in this book will be acquitted, escaping from the verdict and the sentence. Whose names are there and how did they get there?

It is a book that has existed from the beginning of time. It is mentioned in both the Old and New Testaments (Exodus 32:32-33; Philippians 4:3), but most frequently in Revelation (3:5; 13:8; 17:8; 20:12, 15; 21:27; 22:19). God himself writes the names down. It is a list of the people whom he has given to his Son (John 17:6); it is therefore called: *'the Lamb's book of life'* (Revelation 21:27).

How did they qualify for inclusion? They trusted in Christ as their Saviour. They lived by faith. They trusted and obeyed God's words. Their deeds were evidence of their faith. Some names even date back before Christ (Hebrews 11). Abraham is the classic example; his faith, proved by his actions, was *'credited to him as righteousness'* (Genesis 15:6; Psalm 106:31; Romans 4:3; Hebrews 11:8-12; James 2:21-24). Most names come after Christ, as many more trusted and obeyed *'the Word'* whom God had sent.

It must be said that true faith is not a single step but a long walk. It is of the essence of believing in a person to go on believing in them whatever happens. 'Faith' and 'faithfulness' are exactly the same word in both the Hebrew and the Greek languages. *'The righteous shall live by faith'* (Habakkuk 2:4) means *'those whom God reckons as righteous will survive by faithfulness'* (note how this continuity of faith is brought out in Romans 1:17 and Hebrews 10:38-39). The Old Testament heroes of faith were *'still living by faith when they died'* (Hebrews 11:13).

It is possible to depart from the faith, to make shipwreck of it (1 Timothy 1:19-20). It is possible for names in the book of life to be *'blotted out'* as God made clear to Moses (Exodus 32:33). Only those who remain faithful, who *'overcome'* all the pressures to distrust and disobey, will keep their names in until the day the book is finally opened (Revelation 3:5).

These will be acquitted or, to use the term from Roman courts, *'justified'* – not because they are innocent, but because they have *consistently* trusted in Jesus, who has already paid the penalty for their sins. Only because of the cross can God *'be just **and** the one who justifies'* (Romans 3:26). Both his justice and his mercy were fully expressed at Calvary.

With the day of judgement over, the stage is finally set for the redemption of creation. By returning to planet earth the Lord Jesus Christ will have done all that needs to be done to make this possible. He will have completed the saints, converted the Jews, conquered the devil, commanded the world and condemned the ungodly.

A new humanity has been created out of the old race. 'Homo Sapiens' has been replaced by 'Homo Novus'. They are new creatures, part of the new creation. They have not evolved by themselves into this new species; they have been changed by the power of the gospel of God. *'The old man has gone, the new has come'* (2 Corinthians 5:17).

The same thing will now happen to the entire universe. New creatures need a new environment. The 'first' heaven and earth, still bearing the residual damage of angelic and human sin, will pass away (Revelation 21:1). They will be *'destroyed by fire'* (2 Peter 3:10). Since the discovery that every atom is packed with energy that can be released in fire, this scenario becomes entirely credible. From the ashes, like the mythical Phoenix bird, will emerge the new heaven and earth, beautiful beyond imagination.

That the carpenter from Nazareth will be involved in this reconstruction is beyond question. He was engaged in the first creation. Before he made tables and chairs, doors and window frames, he made the trees from which he would later get the timber. Before he preached the Sermon on the Mount, he made the mountain for his pulpit. The wind and the waves obeyed him because they were his handiwork. *'Through him all things were made; without him nothing was made that has been made'* (John 1:3).

Where he (and his) will be during this transformation of the universe, we are not told. So we can only speculate. Maybe in that new metropolitan city of Jerusalem God has designed and built out in space, known about as long ago as the time of Abraham (Hebrews 11:10).

One thing is certain. This vast urban construction, though erected in heaven, will be planted on the new earth (Revelation 21:2, 10). It will be the permanent home of all God's people, Jewish and Gentile.

It will also be the eternal residence for the people's God! Father, Son and Spirit will live *here* with human beings (Revelation 21:3, 23). We are used to thinking of the Son and the Spirit with us, but have always prayed to: *'Our father in heaven'* (Matthew 6:9). We have imagined we would go to heaven and live with him there for ever and ever. But he is coming to earth to live with us! As at the beginning, his footsteps will be heard down here (Genesis 3:8). Even his face will be seen (Revelation 22:4).

All this may seem a little irrelevant to the second coming. Actually it is very significant. Too many Christians have concentrated their attention on heaven. It is the earth which is at the centre of God's purpose in creation and re-creation. It is a renewed earth which will be his and our everlasting home.

The earth is the focus of our expectations for the future. That is the basic reason why Jesus is coming back here to wind up history as we know it. His return to earth is the very hinge of our hope, on which everything else turns.

Perhaps more than any other people, Christians are thoroughly 'down to earth' in their thinking – or should be. In the next section we shall consider how this belief in the future affects behaviour in the present.

2

Making Sure Of
Our Readiness

Why are we told so much about the second coming? We know more about it than any other future event predicted in scripture. There must be a reason.

On the other hand, why are we not told more? Tantalising hints leave us full of unanswered questions. There is so much we'd like to know, but don't.

There must be one explanation to cover both our knowledge and our ignorance, some purpose for which we now know all we need to know, neither too little nor too much.

The purpose is practical. In a word, it is to be *ready* for his return.

Revelation about the future is given to affect the present; not to satisfy mental curiosity, but to stimulate moral consistency; not for information, but for incentive.

We live by hope. That is why it 'springs eternal in the human breast' (to quote Alexander Pope). The future influences the present in all of us. What we believe will happen in the future profoundly affects how we behave now.

This is particularly true of Christians, for whom hope is confident certainty rather than wishful longing (the Greek word ELPIS has this very definite assurance). Sinners are more influenced by their past, with the habits of mind and body. Saints are more influenced by their future, with the hope kindled by the Spirit (Romans 8:23-25). This is a stabilising factor in a changing world, an *'anchor for the soul, firm and secure'* (Hebrews 6:19).

Christians are the people of tomorrow. They are the children of a new age that has already dawned for them and will one day come for the whole world. They look for, long for and live for this cosmic rescue. They may be described as those who have *'turned to God from idols, to serve the living and true God, and to wait for his Son from heaven, whom he raised from the dead – Jesus, who rescues us'* (Colossians 1:9-10).

God has made many promises to send his Son back to complete the deliverance. But the promises are always accompanied by precepts. His people must be ready for the return of their rescuer.

In the New Testament, the hope of Christ's coming is a major motive for godly living in this *'present evil age'*. Even the book of Revelation, containing more predictions than any other, has this practical purpose – not so much that its readers may know what's coming, but that they may be ready for it when it does.

The only time we have to get ready for the future is the present. To delay is to run the risk of being too late.

How, then, can we be ready for his return? There are seven ways.

Individual Faith

'When the Lord Jesus is revealed from heaven in blazing fire with his powerful angels... he will punish those who do not know God and do not obey the gospel of our Lord Jesus' (2 Thessalonians 1:7-8). It is not fanciful to find here two groups among the guilty – those who have not responded rightly to God and those who have not responded rightly to the gospel.

God put men in place on the earth so that they *'would seek him and perhaps reach out for him and find him, though he is not far from each one of us'* (Acts 17:27). To seek means to 'make search or enquiry for, try or be anxious to find or get, ask, aim at, pursue an object, endeavour to do, make for or resort to' (Oxford English Dictionary). Jesus himself exhorted people to *'Go on seeking and you will find... for everyone who goes on seeking does find'* (Luke 11:9-10; I have translated the verb tenses quite literally).

As we have already seen, God has put enough evidence for his power and divinity into creation, the work of his hands, to leave atheists and agnostics *'without any excuse'* (Romans 1:20). Though this is adequate proof of his existence, there are two more requirements to discover his presence.

One is faith. *'And without faith it is impossible to please God because anyone who comes to him must believe that he exists and that he rewards those who earnestly seek him'* (Hebrews 11:6).

The other is repentance. *'Seek the Lord while he may be found; call on him while he is near. Let the wicked forsake his way and the evil man his thoughts. Let him turn to the Lord, and he will have mercy on him, and to our God, for he will freely pardon'* (Isaiah 55:6-7).

Whether there will be many, or even any, who seriously seek God like this, without any knowledge of the gospel, we have no way of knowing. God himself will be the judge of that.

From observation, the general pattern seems to be that human ambition seeks pleasure, wealth, fame, power – everything but God. Human thirst for knowledge covers cooking to computers, DNA to dinosaurs, psychology to sociology – everything but God.

It is unlikely that this book will fall into the hands of someone who has never heard about Jesus, though if it should, they should start looking for God right away. If they don't find him before he finds them out, it would be better for them if they had never been born.

What about those who have heard the gospel? This is an added privilege and responsibility, since we are judged by the light we have received. But it is not enough to have heard it or even to have believed it to be true. The verse with which we began this section talks about *obeying* the gospel. We have to *do* something about it.

Initially, we need to repent and believe, expressing these in an active way by being baptised in water and receiving the Holy Spirit (see my 'Explaining Water Baptism' in this series, or my book 'The Normal Christian Birth', Hodder and Stoughton, 1989). But that is not the end, only the beginning. Alas, many have the impression that, having begun the Christian life, they are now ready for Jesus' return. That would only be the case if his coming immediately followed their conversion (which obviously has not been so for anyone yet!).

The earliest name for the Christian religion was 'The Way' (Acts 18:25-26; 19:9, 23). The gospel is the way to life and a way of life. It cannot be worked for, but it must be worked out (Ephesians 2:9-10; Philippians 2:12-13). After stepping into this 'narrow' way (Matthew 7:14), it is necessary to continue walking in it (Isaiah 30:21; 35:8-10; Ephesians 4:1; 5:2, 8). It is those who are walking with God who are ready to meet him. Enoch is a classic example (Genesis 5:24).

So it is not enough simply to have become a 'believer' in God and in Christ. That is certainly the basic requirement, but Jesus himself made it clear that some believers will be ready for his return and some will not.

What else is necessary?

Continual Service

After giving the signs of his coming to the disciples (in Matthew 24, already expounded), Jesus very significantly went on to the subject of readiness for it (in Matthew 25). He told a number of parables, which are all variations on a single theme: *'so you also must be ready'* (24:44). This urgent imperative is illustrated from different spheres – a household, a wedding, and commercial trading.

The stories have the same plot as well as the same point. In each someone has gone away but is expected to return, though the exact time is not known. It is clear that in the character of the householder, bridegroom and businessman, Jesus was portraying himself. By the same token, those left behind are his followers.

There is the same division of the latter into two types or groups: the wise, who are ready for the return – and the foolish, who are not. Note that 'wise' means sensible rather than clever, and 'foolish' means silly rather than simple.

There is the same test of their readiness. In each parable there is an indication that the return of the key figure is *later* than expected – the bridegroom was *'a long time coming'*, the master returned *'after a long time'*. This is a key point in understanding and applying these stories. The real test is not what people do if they think the return is soon, but what they do if they think it will not be soon (Matthew 24:48). That which is born of persistence is of far more value than that which springs from panic. Real readiness is motivated by the fact of the Lord's return, not its timing.

There is the same virtue in the 'wise' – faithfulness. They behaved the same way in the absence of the key figure as they would in his presence. Even a prolonged absence made no difference; they were fully prepared for that. They proved their trustworthiness. They thus gave joy to the one to whom they were accountable. Their reward was both to share in that pleasure and be promoted to greater responsibility. They 'lived happily ever after'.

There is the same vice in the 'foolish' – negligence. In only one case is a bad thing actually done (the housekeeper bullying the other servants and indulging himself). In the others, it is a case of good things left undone – sins of omission rather than sins of commission, as they have been called, neglected duties. The Bible has a lot to say about the sin of sloth, or laziness, especially in the book of Proverbs (6:6; 10:26; 12:24; 15:19; 19:24; 21:25; 26:15; etc.). It is a serious offence.

Jesus uses very strong language in describing the punishment meted out to such sluggards. *'He will cut him to pieces and assign him a place with the hypocrites, where there will be weeping and gnashing of teeth'* (Matthew 24:51). *'Throw that worthless servant outside into the darkness, where there will be weeping and gnashing of teeth'* (25:30). This is the vocabulary of hell and speaks of the endless regret and remorse in that dreadful place.

Who are these lazy people who have wasted their opportunities? Complacent Christians have too readily identified them as unbelievers. But they are servants in the household, bridesmaids invited to the wedding, employees entrusted with their employer's assets. Such descriptions are far more appropriate to believers. And we need to remember that these parables were not addressed to the general public, but to the twelve disciples – of whom one (Judas) had already shown himself to be untrustworthy, even though he had preached and healed in the name of Jesus.

However, there is more than a hint that behind such unreliability lies a failure in relationship, an inadequate knowledge of the returning person. The wicked servant's claim: *'I knew that you are a hard man...'* (25:24) was rebuked with: 'So you thought you knew me; had you done so, you would also know what I wanted you to do and would have done myself in your place... but you didn't'. To the bridesmaids unprepared for his delay, the bridegroom says: *'I tell you the truth, I don't know you'* (25:12; not, this time: 'You don't know me', which they obviously did; nor even: 'I never knew you', as in Matthew 7:23; but simply, 'I don't recognise you now as having anything to do with me').

Faithful service, then is an essential ingredient in readiness for the Lord's return. It has often been said that the Lord will commend those who have been *faithful*, rather than successful. This is a false dichotomy and has been used to rationalise persistence in useless activity. The Lord wants servants who are both faithful and fruitful, giving him some return on his investment – though even at our best we are still *'unprofitable'* (Luke 17:10).

The quality of our service is also important, not just the quantity. *'If any man builds on this foundation* (Jesus Christ) *using gold, silver, costly stones, wood, hay or straw, his work will be shown for what it is, because the day will bring it to light. It will be revealed with fire and the fire will test the quality of each man's work'* (1 Corinthians 3:12-13). It is not always the busiest who produce the best results.

One further misunderstanding must be dealt with. Faithful service to the Lord is not limited to 'spiritual' activities in our spare time and for the church or gospel. Our daily work can and should be done for the Lord. Adam was a gardener. The Bible evaluates manual labour much more highly than the world does. Shepherding, fishing, tentmaking and carpentry figure prominently. Man was made to work with his hands (Psalm 90:17; 1 Thessalonians 4:11).

The Lord is more interested in *how* we do the job we have than with *what* job we have. He would rather have a conscientious taxi-driver than a careless missionary. He is more concerned about character than career. He must be frustrated to be asked for guidance only when a change of employment is considered.

All work ranks the same with God, as Martin Luther said. Every Christian is in full-time service for the Lord. Every form of employment, provided it is neither illegal nor immoral, is a sacred vocation. In the way we do our daily work, we are writing our future reference, our C.V. ('curriculum vitae', Latin for 'a brief account of one's previous career'). On it will depend our role and responsibility in the kingdom set up by Christ at his coming.

He will look for dependability, not just ability. He will employ those to whom he can say: *'Well done, good and faithful servant! You have been faithful with a few things; I will put you in charge of many things. Come and share your master's happiness'* (Matthew 25:21 23).

Personal Holiness

The gospel is good news about holiness, as well as forgiveness. It is not just an offer of forgiveness and a demand for holiness – a widespread impression, often fostered by preachers. Both are an offer. It is now possible to have sins conquered as well as cancelled. We can have the ability as well as the appetite to live right, to be righteous.

Gifts must be received. Both forgiveness and holiness are available, but both need to be appropriated. Too many claim one without the other. They want to be justified now and sanctified later!

Of course, they will be. *'We know that when he appears, we shall be like, him, for we shall see him as he is'* (1 John 3:2). When we meet him in our new glorious bodies, we shall be perfect, complete, totally transformed in every part of our being. At last we shall live up to the title he gave us when we began to follow him: *'saints'* (Romans 1:7; 2 Corinthians 1:1; Ephesians 1:1; etc.). The word means 'holy ones'.

But John draws a very practical implication from this future expectancy. *'Everyone who has this hope in him purifies himself, even as he is pure'* (1 John 3:3). In other words, if we are really convinced that our future destiny is to be holy, this belief will be evidenced in our present behaviour.

It would be quite unnatural for someone expecting to inherit a large fortune not to want as much of it as possible as quickly as possible. If part of it could be obtained in advance, they would surely apply for it, especially if they were in real need of it.

In other words, it is a question of genuine desire. If we really welcome the hope of being utterly Christlike one day, we will pursue that goal right now. We will have no desire *'to enjoy the pleasures of sin for a short time'* (Hebrews 11:25).

We will want to be holy here and now, if that is possible. And it is possible, though its achievement will be neither easy nor quick. It will involve 'effort', that combination of energy, enthusiasm and endurance.

Frequent thoughts about 'the Day' when we look into his face and his eyes look into ours, provides the incentive. Those who have made little effort to be holy, revealing no real desire to be, will be deeply embarrassed, unable to meet his penetrating gaze. How terrible to have him say: 'I could have done so much with you, but you didn't want me to'.

Again, we must emphasise that it is those who persevere who will be approved. *'And now, dear children, continue in him, so that when he appears we may be confident and unashamed before him at his coming'* (1 John 2:28).

The New Testament grounds its appeal for many qualities of sainthood on the fact of Jesus' return. Sobriety, fidelity, moderation, patience, sincerity, obedience, diligence, purity, godliness, brotherly love – all these and more are stimulated by the thought of seeing Jesus again. This appeal becomes particularly effective when believers are collectively represented as a bride for whom the bridegroom is coming.

Jesus was not married during his first visit to earth, but will be at his second! In a very real sense, believers are only 'betrothed', engaged to Christ in the present. When he returns, the relationship will be consummated and celebrated in *'the wedding supper of the Lamb'* (Revelation 19:9; cf. Matthew 22:2).

This metaphor runs right through the Bible. It is applied as much to Israel in the Old Testament as to the Church in the New. God's covenant with his people is seen in terms of a marriage vow. The metaphor of bride and groom is applied in two different ways.

Negatively, unfaithfulness is seen as adultery, even prostitution. If committed during betrothal, that was grounds for divorce, which nearly happened to the mother of Jesus! (Matthew 1:19). To prepare for a wedding is to preserve one's virginity. A bride to be will keep herself only for her future bridegroom. *'I promised you to one husband, to Christ, so that I might present you as a pure virgin to him'* (2 Corinthians 11:2).

Positively, a bride will also be concerned about her appearance at the wedding as well as her abstinence before it. The Church will want to be what Christ wants for her on that day: *'to present her to himself as a radiant church, without stain or wrinkle or any other blemish, but holy and blameless'* (Ephesians 5:27).

This will include her clothes as well as her complexion. Clothing figures in a number of statements about the second coming. *'Behold, I come like a thief! Blessed is he who stays awake and keeps his clothes with him, so that he may not go naked and be shamefully exposed'* (Revelation 16:15). Even the desire to be married in white, the symbol of purity, has its moral counterpart: *'For the wedding of the Lamb has come, and his bride has made herself ready. Fine linen, bright and clean, was given her to wear. (Fine linen stands for the righteous acts of the saints)'* (Revelation 19:7-8). Note the balance between *'given her'* and *'made herself ready'*. Clothes may be a gift, but they must be put on and worn at the wedding. Jesus told a parable to warn those invited to participate but who don't bother to change that hell awaits such presumption (Matthew 22:11-13).

It is therefore essential to *'make every effort to live in peace with all men and to be holy; without holiness no-one will see the Lord'* (Hebrews 12:14). Only by so doing will *'your whole spirit, soul and body be kept blameless at the coming of our Lord Jesus Christ'* (1 Thessalonians 5:23).

Communal Fellowship

Holiness, or wholeness, has a corporate as well as an individual application. The 'bride' is one person as well as many. *'Christ loved the church and gave himself up for her to make her holy'* (Ephesians 5:25-26).

Believers are called to be *'a chosen people, a royal priesthood, a holy nation, a people belonging to God'* (1 Peter 2:9). They are to demonstrate a corporate identity in a decadent world, a convincing unity in a divided world. Jesus wants to find such a people on his return. What are the implications?

At the very least, it means that Christians must not isolate themselves from other believers. *'Let us not give up meeting together, as we are in the habit of doing, but let us encourage one another – and all the more as you see the Day approaching'* (Hebrews 10:25). There is safety in numbers and, as pressures on God's people increase toward the end, it will be vital to stay together.

There is a responsibility for mutual service, as well as moral support. Servants have duties to each other, as well as to their master. Jesus spoke of a servant given the task of feeding his fellow servants during his master's absence. He not only neglected this task, but was guilty of drunken assaults on them. At the master's return, he was thrown into hell for abusing his position in this way (Matthew 24:45-51).

On the same occasion, Jesus told the 'parable' of the sheep and the goats (actually, it is not a parable at all but a predictive prophecy containing an analogy). *'When the Son of man comes in his glory, and all the angels with him, he will sit on his throne in heavenly glory. All the nations will be gathered before him, and he will separate the people one from another **as** a shepherd separates the sheep from the goats'* (Matthew 25:31-32).

The principle of judgement is whether *'the least of these my brethren'* were cared for in a practical way, whether their needs were met and their trials shared. Of course, the application depends on the interpretation of *'my brethren'*. Who are they? To say they are Jesus' fellow-countrymen, the Jews, is too narrow. To say they are his fellow-humans, the whole race, is too broad. The title is consistently applied to his disciples, out of all nations (Matthew 12:49; 28:10; cf. Hebrews 22:11). It is the neglect of his disciples that qualifies the rejected 'goats' on his left hand.

That this group could include some of the disciples themselves is indicated by their calling Jesus 'lord' (Matthew 25:44; cf. 7:21) and by the fact that this 'parable' was not spoken to the general public, but to his inner circle of the twelve. The theme of negligence among his own followers runs through all the parables in this chapter, as does the awful penalty to be paid for it.

Positively, the 'sheep' are those who have ministered to his brethren, even 'the least' significant of them, in their hour of need. They have been motivated by love of the brethren, without even thinking that it was as good as doing it for Jesus himself (Matthew 25:37-38). Their deeds were acts of compassionate spontaneity, not calculated self-interest.

The need to be ready covers the church as a whole, as well as its individual members. Those who truly hope for his return will want as much holiness as is attainable now for all his people, as well as for themselves.

They will have a concern for the *unity* of the Church. When all are gathered to meet their Lord in the air, all differences will fade into insignificance. Denominational labels, liturgical styles, ecclesiastical structures, theological arguments – all will disappear from sight when we see his face. There will be an atmosphere of total harmony on that Day, which will be reflected in united worship.

Whoever has this hope will both want and work for an anticipation of it here and now. They will take seriously the prayer Jesus prayed on the last evening before his death, which was precisely for just such a demonstration of what was to come (John 17:20-24).

Of course, unity must be defined his way. It is neither union nor uniformity but the unanimity of heart, mind and will, such as he had with his Father. It is based on truth rather than tolerance. Those who seek it will not be indifferent to things that are wrong.

They will have a concern for the *purity* of the Church. In matters of belief and behaviour, they will seek to cleanse defiled churches and keep them consistent with the gospel they preach. This will involve confrontation and conflict (1 Corinthians 11:19).

How significant it is that the book of Revelation, whose whole message centres on the second coming, should open with commands to local churches to deal with heresy and immorality in their midst. The threat of punishment is matched by the promise of rewards at his return (Revelation 2:10, 25-26; 3:5, 11). However, while whole churches may be 'removed' for not putting things right, the rewards are offered to individual members who seek to do something about it. Anyone can open the Church door to let Jesus back in (Revelation 3:20, a verse that has nothing to do with personal regeneration and everything to do with communal restoration).

This joint concern for the unity and purity of God's people as a whole is an essential ingredient in readiness for his return. The bride, which is his Church, needs to *'make herself ready'* (Revelation 19:7).

Global Evangelism

It has been rightly said that the Church is the only society on earth that exists primarily for the sake of its non-members! She has a task to be completed before Jesus returns; indeed, before he *can* come back. *'This gospel of the kingdom will be preached in the whole world as a testimony to all nations, and then the end will come'* (Matthew 24:14). There is even a possibility that tackling this task with urgency and enthusiasm could *'speed its coming'* (2 Peter 3:12; though the verb can be translated 'wait eagerly' as well as 'hasten', and the context is not mission).

All four Gospels conclude with this 'Great Commission' to the apostles (Matthew 28:18-20; Mark 16:15-18; Luke 24:47-48; John 20:21-23) – and through them to the Church throughout time and space, since the twelve could not possibly complete the job themselves. The gospel is to be preached to every creature and disciples made of every 'nation' (this means ethnic groups, not political states).

It is God' desire and intention to have within his family, the new humanity living on the new earth, men and women *'from every tribe and language and people and nation'* (Revelation 5:10; 7:9). He made them all *'from one man'* (Acts 17:26) and will merge their variety into unity again by bringing them *'together under one head, even Christ'* (Ephesians 1:10). We are not encouraged to believe that whole nations will be saved; the objective is to 'save' some from every nation.

So the mission is worldwide, *'to the ends of the earth'* (Acts 1:8; cf. Isaiah 45:22; 49:6; 52:10). Not until every corner of our planet has heard the good news in its own language will the work be finished.

The approach of the twenty-first century, the third millennium since Jesus was here, has stimulated a renewed interest in evangelism by reminding us how long it is taking us to complete the task he gave us and how little time may be left to do so.

However the passing of time should not be our main motive. It should be enough that we have been commanded by our Lord to do this. The simple obligation of obedience is always relevant. But gratitude to the Lord for our own salvation will do more than stimulate a willingness to do what he tells us to do. It will also give us a burning desire to share what we have found with those who are 'lost', whether they know it or not. *'For Christ's love compels us'* (2 Corinthians 5:14). This was said by a man who felt himself under a curse if he kept such good news to himself: *'Woe to me if I do not preach the gospel'* (1 Corinthians 9:16).

Quite simply, those who are really looking forward to meeting Christ personally when he returns will not be content to come alone. They will want to bring as many others with them as possible.

Those who are most ready will do most to get others ready! They will be inspired by the thought of making it possible for more to share in the sheer joy of living with God in a brand new earth. They will also be influenced by the horror of their destiny if they do not hear and respond. This urgency will not lead them into offensive methods which are counter-productive in communicating the message; but it will alert them to every opportunity for doing so with a love that is wise and sensitive.

The joy of introducing others to faith in Christ now is just a foretaste of what we shall feel when we see them meeting him face to face. And if the angels celebrate now when just one sinner repents (Luke 15:7, 10), what will they be like 'when the saints go marching in'?

Social Action

It is now generally accepted that evangelism and social action belong together in the mission of the Church, though many would rightly give priority to the former.

There is a clear biblical basis for service to an unbelieving world. Jesus endorsed the second 'great' commandment to love our neighbours as ourselves (Mark 12:31); and he interpreted 'neighbour' to cover anyone in need whom we can help (Luke 10:29-37). Paul exhorts us: *'Therefore, as we have opportunity, let us do good to all people'* (Galatians 6:10); he adds: *'especially to those who belong to the family of believers'*). Though it is the most common scripture quoted in this connection, we have already noted that the so-called 'parable' of the sheep and goats is not strictly relevant, since 'brethren' and 'neighbour' are not equivalent terms; but the case should not rest on that passage.

Let it be clearly stated that we are not saved *by* doing good deeds (a widespread but mistaken notion) but we are saved *for* doing good deeds (Ephesians 2:9-10). We are saved to serve – and to serve indiscriminately whoever needs us, whatever their relationship or response to us. Such unconditional love has a special word in Greek: *AGAPE* (pronounced 'agapay'). Infrequently used in the ancient world, it came into its own when describing God's love for the world expressed in Christ and the consequent love exercised by Christians, both of which included even enemies.

Love of neighbours can be applied at three levels of social activity.

First, in work, Provided it is meeting a real need in society, our daily work can and should be seen as a practical expression of neighbourly love. So often it is regarded as a means to our own ends – to get money, status or satisfaction for ourselves. Actually, it is far more likely to be fulfilling, as God intended it to be, if we see it primarily as a way of helping others. Obviously, this is easier with some jobs (nursing, for example) than others (repetitive factory operations) but they can all be done to meet a need, to benefit people.

Second, in welfare, Christians have a good record in voluntary service to the distressed. They have pioneered care of the sick, the elderly, the handicapped and those who have been abandoned to their fate by a selfish society. James, Jesus' brother, has stimulated much of it with his definition: *'Religion that God our father accepts as pure and faultless is this: to look after orphans and widows in their distress and to keep oneself from being polluted by the world'* (James 1:27; note that active philanthropy is no substitute for moral integrity).

Third, in reform. It is at this point that Christians have real differences. There is unanimity over relieving suffering, but not over reforming systems. For this involves political activity, at local or national level. This is so often a matter of compromise, especially under democracy, constantly finding a mean between moral absolutes and material necessities, between what is ideally applicable and what is socially acceptable (reducing the period of pregnancy in which abortion can take place is a typical example).

While acknowledging that legislation cannot impose good, it can restrain evil – and therefore reduce suffering. To relieve the exploited or oppressed victims of an evil system is one thing. To seek to change the system itself is another. It is a less direct and more impersonal way of dealing with the problem. But if it achieves the same end, relief of suffering, and perhaps on a greater scale, can this not also express love of our neighbour?

Paul exhorts us to do good to *all* people, *'as we have opportunity'* (Galatians 6:10). Christians who are in a position of responsibility for others, in commerce and industry, in civil service and politics, have such an 'opportunity' to change the system for the better.

They will be aware of the danger of imposing distinctively 'godly' behaviour with legal sanctions (for example, to observe Sunday as a holy day or holiday). But they will seek just laws that counter inhumanity. It was for such things that the Hebrew prophets denounced the nations outside Israel, not for breaking the laws given to the redeemed people of God (for example, Amos 1:3–2:3).

Those who believe in a millennial reign of Christ on earth after his return are highly motivated for social reform. As with the hope for perfected individuals and a perfected Church, the expectation of a perfected society stimulates the desire to claim as much of this as possible in the here and now. The certainty that one day there will be a perfect world order, spurs them to greater efforts to work for peace and justice now.

Not that they hope to achieve his, either on a universal or even national scale, before the King returns to set up his kingdom. But they can at least demonstrate the nature of that kingdom by applying its principles to contemporary situations. This in itself commends *'the gospel of the kingdom'* (Matthew 24:14).

It is even more personal and practical than that. If the world is to be governed by Christians *'reigning with Christ'* and public offices are to be in their hands (for example, the law courts, 1 Corinthians 6:2), then the more experience they can gain in these positions of responsibility the better.

Let us close this section with an example of one such believer in the nineteenth century.

In the west end of London, Piccadilly Circus to be precise, stands an aluminium statue. Its resemblance to Cupid, the agent of love, has given it the popular nickname 'EROS' (the Greek word for sex appeal, from which we derive 'erotic'). This is grossly misleading. It should be called 'AGAPE'. It represents the angel of mercy and is a memorial to Anthony Ashley Cooper, better known as Lord Shaftesbury.

He did more perhaps than anyone else in his day to relieve the suffering caused by the 'Industrial Revolution', which transferred a huge population from rural to urban areas, putting them to work in factories and mines under unhealthy, even inhumane, circumstances. They were simply 'hands' to be exploited by unscrupulous employers. His tactics were to arouse sufficient guilt in public opinion to enable legislation to be passed which limited the potential abuse.

Few are aware that behind these public endeavours lay a constant and conscious expectation of Christ's return to rule for which he sought to be ready. At the top of every letter he wrote were the words: *'Even so, come, Lord Jesus'*, a prayer to be found on the last page of the Bible (Revelation 22:20).

Loyal Endurance

Is the world likely to get better or worse? At the beginning of the twentieth century, the general opinion was optimistic; the key word was 'progress'. Now at the end of it, the outlook is pessimistic; the key word is 'survival'.

Christian and Communist share an 'apocalyptic' view of history. They both got it from Jewish sources, where it originated – one through Jesus Christ and the other through Karl Marx.

Simply put, two future phases of history are anticipated. First, things will get much worse before they get better. Second, things will get much better after they get worse. This is the basic structure of the book of Revelation (in chapters 4–17 the situation gets worse; in chapters 18–22 it gets better).

As things get bad in the world, it gets even worse for God's people in the world. Indirectly, they suffer the general troubles, but in the 'Great Tribulation' at the end they will suffer specific attacks directed at them, primarily because of their refusal to submit to a totalitarian regime with divine pretensions.

Many will pay the price with their own blood. The number of martyrs will rapidly increase as the climax approaches. Indeed, at times the book of Revelation seems to assume that nearly all believers will die for their faith, so that 'overcomers' and 'martyrs' are almost synonymous. It is significant that the Greek word MARTUS or MARTUR originally meant 'witness', but now means someone who maintains a faithful testimony at the cost of life itself.

But there has been a 'noble army of martyrs' for nearly two thousand years, ever since the stoning of Stephen (Acts 7:54-66). Not a decade has passed without people dying for their faith in Jesus. The coming 'Big Trouble' or 'Great Tribulation' may be on a wider scale than ever before, but it has already been experienced at local and even national levels.

In the godless world, suffering is one of the sure signs of a genuine disciple. *'Everyone who wants to live a godly life in Christ Jesus will be persecuted'* (2 Timothy 3:12). The early Church taught its converts to expect trouble (Acts 14:22). They even counted it an honour (Acts 5:31). After all, Jesus had promised it: *'In this world you will have trouble'* (John 16:33).

What enables believers to survive such pressures, even to overcome them and be *'more than conquerors'* (Romans 8:37)? It is their sure hope of his return, when they will receive their reward and share his reign. Not least will be their public vindication in the eyes of the world that expelled them.

The New Testament is full of such encouragement. One of the favourite sayings of the early Church was: *'If we died with him, we will also live with him; if we endure, we will also reign with him'* (2 Timothy 3:11). Martyrs will sit on thrones (Revelation 20:4). They will wear crowns given to those are are *'faithful, even to the point of death'* (Revelation 22:10). Paul, awaiting execution, knew he would be entitled to one: *'I have fought the good fight, I have finished the race, I have kept the faith. Now there is in store for me the crown of righteousness, which the Lord, the righteous judge, will award to me on that day'* (1 Timothy 4:8).

Overcomers will be heaped with rewards – the right to eat from the tree of life, the hidden manna, the white stone, a new name, authority over the nations, the morning star, white robes, a permanent position in God's temple and many more (Revelation 2:7, 17, 26; 3:5, 12).

All this will be theirs at his coming. In that perspective, suffering is reduced to size and loses its power to intimidate. *'For our light and momentary troubles are achieving for us an eternal glory that far outweighs them all'* (2 Corinthians 4:17).

As well as these positive incentives, there is also a negative deterrent associated with his coming. The 'faithful saying' already quoted continues: *'If we disown him, he will also disown us'* (2 Timothy 2:12). This warning is based on Jesus' own words: *'But whoever disowns me before men, I will disown him before my Father in heaven'* (Matthew 10:33).

This is precisely the danger addressed in the letter to the Hebrews. Believing Jews were tempted to leave the Church and return to the synagogue in order to avoid the growing persecution of the Christians. To be accepted back they would be required to renounce belief that Jesus was their Messiah. They are warned that it is impossible to repent of such apostasy (Hebrews 6:4-6; cf.

2:1; 3:12-34; 10:26). When he returns, Jesus will *'not be pleased'* with those who shrink back (literally, 'lower their sails') – and are destroyed (Hebrews 10:37-38).

The book of Revelation is full of such warnings. The 'cowardly' will have their names blotted out of the Lamb's book of life and be thrown into the lake of fire (Revelation 3:5; 22:8). The everlasting torment awaiting those who give in to the pressures of hostile authorities calls for patient endurance on the part of the saints who obey God's commandments and remain faithful to Jesus (Revelation 14:12). The whole book is addressed to believers about to face such a test of their faith and is intended to enable them to come through it with flying colours. Perhaps this is why readers not facing such a crisis find the book difficult to understand!

When persecution breaks out, few things enable believers to endure as much as the conviction that Jesus will come to vanquish the oppressor and vindicate the oppressed. They know that *'he who stands firm to the end will be saved'* (Matthew 24:13).

These, then, are the ways to be ready for his return – individual faith, continual service, personal holiness, communal fellowship, global evangelism, social action and loyal endurance.

Facing such an agenda, many may feel daunted, even discouraged. Let us remember that the issue is not whether we have reached these goals by the time he comes, but whether we are still pressing on towards them (Philippians 3:14).

Can we ever reach the stage when we know we are ready? There is one very simple measure of this, namely: how soon we want him to come!

True believers not only *'wait for his Son from heaven'* (1 Thessalonians 1:10). They long for his appearing (2 Timothy 4:8; literally, 'having loved his appearing'). They not only have thoughts about it. They have feelings about it. They yearn, even pine, for that day. They wish it could be tomorrow at the latest, today if possible.

As a bride, preparing for her marriage, longs for the day of the wedding, wishing it could be brought forward, so the Church should look forward to the bridegroom's return. *'The Spirit and the bride say, come!'* (Revelation 22:17). How many romantic novels have ended with the words: 'so they got married and lived happily ever after'. The Bible is no exception!

The shortest prayer in the early church was composed of two words in the Aramaic language: 'MARANA THA'. It means simply: *'Lord, come!'* Perhaps the best indication of our readiness to meet him is the frequency with which the phrase, in whatever language, comes spontaneously into our minds and out of our mouths.

It seems appropriate to conclude our study with some wise words of Augustine, many centuries ago: 'He who loves the coming of the Lord is not he who affirms it is far off, nor is it he who says it is near; but rather he who, whether it be far off or near, awaits it with sincere faith, steadfast hope and fervent love'.

A Word Of Explanation

Within the compass of a booklet this size, it has only been possible to hint at how I reached my conclusions or why I hold these convictions. It has likewise been impossible to consider other views on many of the related issues.

To put it another way, this material represents what I have said in the pulpit, rather than what I have done in my study. An impression could be given that I have neither recognised nor researched those aspects where others would take quite a different view from the one given here. Two examples may be given:

I do not believe that Christians will be secretly snatched out of the world before the 'Great Tribulation'. I do believe that Christ will reign on this earth for a thousand years.

While this 'post-tribulation, pre-millennial' view of the second coming seems to have been generally held in the early Church for the first few centuries, it is far less common today. I believe it is the truest to scripture, though I have not had the space to argue the case.

This is covered in a forthcoming volume entitled 'When Jesus Returns' (published by Hodder and Stoughton), of which one section will consist of the material presented here. I am grateful to both publishers for agreeing to this.

The larger volume will be for those who wish to study the subject in greater depth, with a view to reaching, reinforcing or revising their own convictions.

In addition to the two most controversial questions of the 'Rapture' and the 'Millenium', there will be a more thorough consideration of the Old Testament prophecies, the Kingdom in the teaching of Jesus, the future of Israel and the biblical philosophy of history. These have only lightly been touched upon in the present work, as careful readers will have noticed.

Finally, there will be a whole section on how to interpret the book of Revelation, the source of so much information and so much variation in understanding the Second Coming. I believe a fresh approach is needed.

I hope this has whetted your appetite. Why not decide to pursue your study by obtaining that more comprehensive book – and give this one away to someone who will benefit from it? That would help both of you to increase your understanding of this vital subject.